Michael Powell

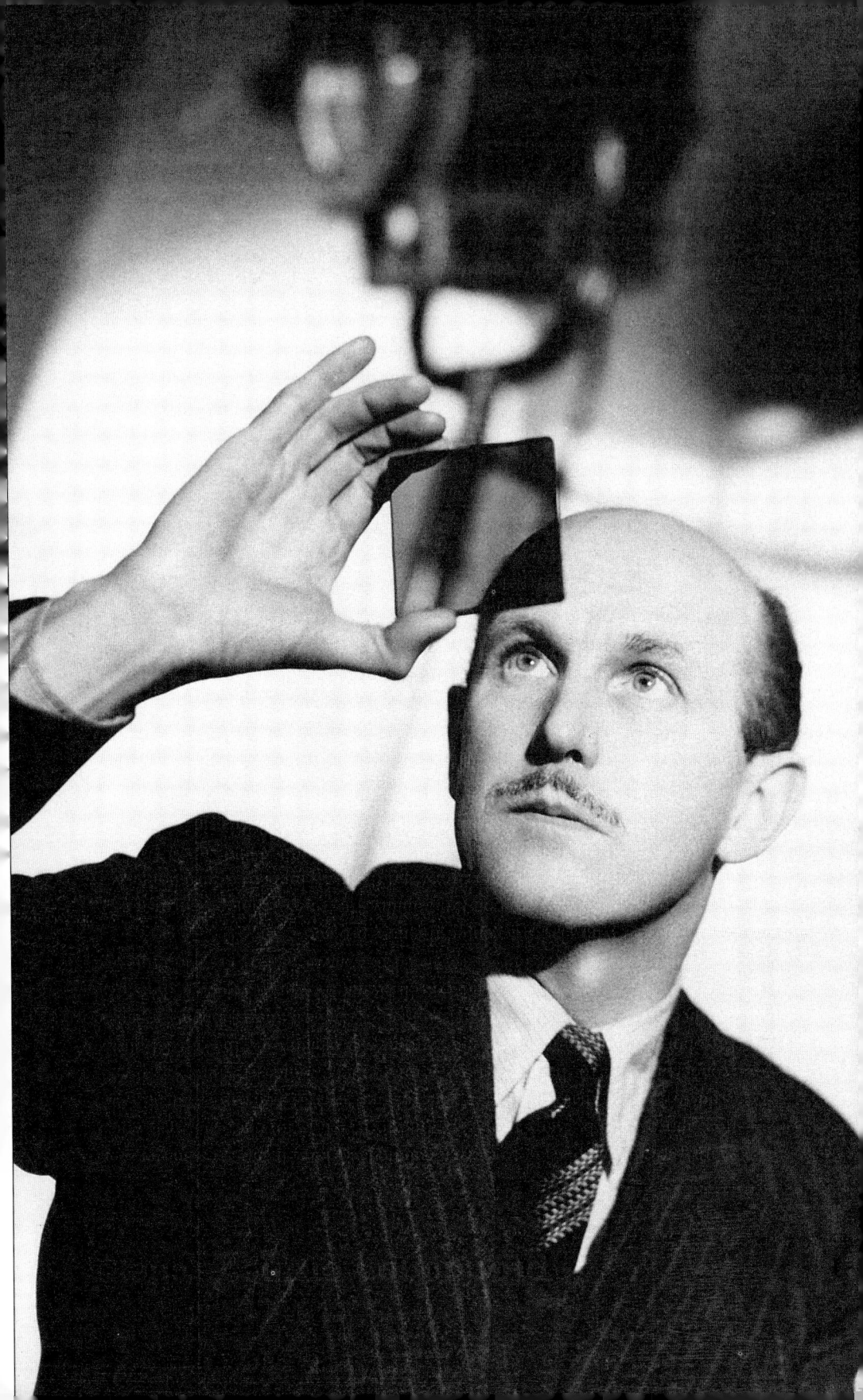

Michael Powell

James Howard

B T Batsford Ltd, London

First published 1996
© James Howard 1996

Printed in Great Britain by Butler and Tanner

for the publishers
BT Batsford Ltd
4 Fitzhardinge Street
London W1H 0AH

A CIP catalogue record for this book is available from the British Library

ISBN 0 7134 7482 3

Contents

Acknowledgements

To my dear parents, Violet and Joseph for their constant support and encouragement throughout everything. Love you both always.

My thanks to Timothy Auger and Richard Reynolds of BT Batsford Ltd., David Thompson (BBC TV), Ian Brown (Thames Television) and, for their time, generous help and courtesy: Robert Arden, Renée Asherson, Maxine Audley, Robert Beatty, Sir Dirk Bogarde, Brenda Bruce, Christopher Challis, Petula Clark, Cyril Cusack, Bryan Forbes, Rumer Godden, Stewart Granger, Dame Wendy Hiller, Kim Hunter, Deborah Kerr, Ursula Le Guin, Jenny Laird, Anna Massey, Daniel Massey, Thelma Schoonmaker Powell, John Schlesinger, Sebastian Shaw, Moira Shearer, Michael Winner and Googie Withers.

As always, I am indebted to the British Film Institute's invaluable research library and reading room, Stills, Posters and Design Department and Briony Dickson of Viewing Services. Stills and illustrations from the National Film Archive collection were originally produced to promote films made and distributed by London Films, the Rank Organisation, BFI Distribution and UK Film Distributors, to whom acknowledgement is duly made. Apologies are offered for any unintentional omission or error.

Thanks to the publishers for their kind permission to quote from the following sources:

A House with Four Rooms (1989) by Rumer Godden, published by Macmillan.

Before I Forget (1981) by James Mason, published by Hamish Hamilton.

Life With Googie (1979) by John McCallum, published by Heinemann.

A Life in Movies (1985) and *Million Dollar Movie* (1992) by Michael Powell. Reprinted by permission of the publisher William Heinemann Ltd and the estate of Michael Powell.

Edge of the World by Michael Powell (original title *20,000 Feet on Foula*) published under this title by Faber and Faber (1990).

Wartime memos relating to *Colonel Blimp* are Crown copyright, held at the Public Records Office (file PREM 4 14/15).

And – corny as it may be – last, but of course by no means least, my love as always to my wife Susie, without whom…

Foreword

I am delighted to have been asked to write a brief foreword to James Howard's book, *Michael Powell*.

Michael Powell and Emeric Pressburger formed their company The Archers and were responsible for some of the most outstanding films made in England. I was doubly fortunate in playing in two of their most remarkable works: *The Life and Death of Colonel Blimp* and *Black Narcissus.*

Michael Powell was a brilliant and imaginative director, and Emeric Pressburger his equally imaginative and brilliant writer. They complemented each other to perfection. How I wish they were both with us to enjoy the praise of their work!

Deborah Kerr

● 'You might say that she was my ideal'.
Deborah Kerr in *The Life and Death of Colonel Blimp* (1943).

● Eric Portman in the lecture sequence in *A Canterbury Tale* (1944).

Introduction

There can have been no more British film-maker than Michael Powell, whose active cinema career stretched over half a century, almost from the very beginnings of popular cinema itself.

A chance meeting in France in 1925 introduced Powell to the film business and, on returning to England, he soon became one of the most prolific – though not yet necessarily the best – of the British directors at work on an endless stream of 'quota quickies' whose shooting schedules measured in days and ludicrously low budgets were often all too apparent on screen.

It is easy to dismiss these films as inconsequential, as Powell later did. Easy, too, to hail them as early milestones in the *oeuvre* of the future cinematic master. In truth, the quality of the 23 films made over this five-year period varies wildly. Like other British features of the era – including minor classics such as *The Ghost Camera* and *Death on the Set* – some retain great charm, while others were all too obviously produced as quickly and cheaply as possible as a straight job of work. Often ingeniously made (given the budget restraints), there is little in these 'quickies' – other than the striking location work in *The Phantom Light*, later to be amplified in the Scottish trilogy *The Edge of the World, The Spy in Black* and *I Know Where I'm Going!* – to suggest the direction which Powell's work was to take.

With the Hungarian Emeric Pressburger – it often takes a non-Englishman to pinpoint the British character accurately – Powell's Archers Productions observed varied aspects of being British, though not always to unanimous critical acclaim. A celebration of the British countryside and its heritage (*A Canterbury Tale*) was savaged by critics, while an affectionate portrait of a blustering old gentleman soldier (*The Life and Death of Colonel Blimp*) brought on its creators the wrath of a government led by no less a figure than Winston Churchill. Yet these were British preoccupations: the beauty of the island and the quirks and curiosities of its people.

Powell's films could be tough (*49th Parallel*), romantic (*I Know Where I'm Going!*), exotic (*Black Narcissus*), realistic (*One of Our*

Aircraft is Missing), topical (*Contraband*), intensely fantastic (*The Red Shoes*), grittily thrilling (*The Small Back Room*), dazzling (*A Matter of Life and Death*) or shocking (*Peeping Tom*), but all were shot through with an indefineable sense of humour and the eye of a poet.

The waywardness in his choice of film subjects – often labelled 'vulgar' or 'tasteless' – left Michael Powell a less accessible figure than the much-fêted Alfred Hitchcock, so that while the latter was honoured with a knighthood in 1969, despite having become an American citizen some years earlier, neither Powell nor Pressburger ever received official recognition in Britain.

When Hitchcock – Powell's near contemporary – left for America at the first opportunity in 1939, he gained international prestige, larger budgets and improved studio facilities and production values. He also sacrificed a great deal of artistic freedom, being often forced to accept studio contract stars against his wishes, while his films lost much of their humour and charm – compare *The 39 Steps* or *Young and Innocent* with *Under Capricorn, The Paradine Case* or the overlong remake of *The Man Who Knew Too Much.*

Although he considered making the same move in 1937, Powell remained in England where the Archers' films inevitably attracted less international interest, although *The Red Shoes* and *Black Narcissus* were among the most honoured of British films by the American Academy. As writers/producers/directors, Powell and Pressburger retained total control over their productions, each of which was recognizably of their making.

By the time Michael Powell finally reached Hollywood in 1980 it was altogether too late. At 75 he was too old (for insurance purposes), the business conglomerate-led studios had no place for such a maverick, and there was no Emeric Pressburger at his side. His best offer – as an advisor to Francis Ford Coppola – ended with the collapse of Coppola's adventurous but ultimately doomed Zoetrope studios.

The enforced idleness of Powell's final decade and the frankly inferior quality of late efforts such as *The Queen's Guards* and *Honeymoon* did little to damage his reputation among the British film community. Writer/director Bryan Forbes, who made his screen acting debut in *The Small Back Room,* insists 'Michael was one of the last great stylists… In the heyday of British films immediately after the war, he was always at the forefront and produced, to my mind, a series of original films that were certainly distinguished even when they failed to completely hit the target'.

Other British film-makers value Powell equally highly. John Schlesinger also acted for Powell in a couple of pictures before becoming a director himself. 'I have always been a tremendous admirer of his films', he says. 'He truly extended the boundaries of that medium at a time when the British cinema badly needed it'. Fellow director Michael Winner recalls Powell as 'undoubtedly our most innovative and brilliant motion picture director. He combined very human stories with extraordinary imagination and flair. They were the sort of films that just could not be made today, and even in his time were unlike any other films being made'. Winner adds mischievously, 'Of course his films were in a way too good for the public...'.

Stewart Granger – 'of course I was a great admirer of Micky Powell. I was sorry I never had the pleasure of being in one of his films' – shared Powell's own theory concerning the seemingly insurmountable obstacles the director faced in later years. 'His career would have continued much longer if he hadn't fallen foul of that nasty John Davis – Rank's man – a monster. Like me, Michael said what he thought... He, Carol Reed and Hitchcock were the giants of the British cinema'.

Many others also place Powell alongside Hitchcock and Carol Reed as the three greatest directors Britain has yet produced. Hitchcock, it has already been noted, cannot truly be claimed as a British director at all from 1939 onwards. Carol Reed's early career had promised much, reaching its peak between 1946 and 1951 (*Odd Man Out, The Fallen Idol, The Third Man, Outcast of the Islands*), but much of his later work – including *The Agony and the Ecstasy, Trapeze* and the hugely successful *Oliver!* – bears no great directorial stamp and could have been made by almost anybody.

Unlike with either Reed or Hitchcock, at the time of Powell's death there was still the feeling that he could have achieved even more in the years to come. Of the three, Powell remains the most idiosyncratic, remarkable (and British!) of British film-makers, and, particularly during his collaboration with Emeric Pressburger, made more great films than was fully appreciated at the time but which are now finally recognized as national treasures.

1

Early years and 'quota quickies'

For his entry in *Who's Who*, Michael Powell gave as his favourite recreation activity 'leaning on gates'. An example of Powell's quirky sense of humour perhaps, although he probably spent much of the last 10 years of his life doing just that rather than working on movies; a depressing situation for probably Britain's greatest director whose best films are landmarks of British and world cinema, many of them restored, reissued and 'rediscovered' a half-century later. The overworked phrase is for once true: they were 'ahead of their time'.

Michael Latham Powell was born near Canterbury, England on 30 September 1905. It was an area which he loved and which provided the setting of probably his most personal – and misunderstood – film, *A Canterbury Tale*, almost 40 years later. Powell would be forever grateful to be born a 'Man of Kent'.

Young Micky – Powell was always 'Micky' to family and friends – spent his childhood on a country farm with mother Mabel, elder brother John and hop farming father Thomas. Tom Powell was also a gambler and a good season's crop paid for his regular trips to the casinos of Monte Carlo. Micky's education at King's School, Canterbury was 'violently interrupted' in 1914 by the outbreak of the First World War which split the Powell family as it did so many others. Tom Powell did not return in 1918, but unlike many less fortunate veterans of the battlefields, this was due to his decision to settle in France where he bought a share in a hotel.

Holidays in France became a part of the family routine, and it was during one of these that Powell saw his earliest remembered movies – *Fantomas* and *The Three Musketeers* – apparently affecting him no more than any other young matinee-goer. However, after seeing D.W. Griffith's *Intolerance* in England in 1921, he spotted a copy of the first-ever issue of *Picturegoer* magazine containing articles on the making of that film. From then on, he would be hooked on the movie-making process.

The family finally pulled up roots and headed for France and another hotel on the Riviera at St Jean Cap Ferrat, but parental disputes soon led to an inevitable divorce. Michael – now an only child following the death of his brother John at the age of 15 – returned with his mother to England and his first job as a bank clerk, impatiently waiting for the holidays when he could return to his father's hotel, *La Voile d'Or*. On one such visit, Powell senior effected an introduction for his son to a film crew working near the hotel, and in 1925, Tom made the acquaintance of an MGM unit on location under the direction of the great Rex Ingram (real name Rex Ingram Montgomery Hitchcock – a coincidence which would assume further significance for Powell a few years later). Young Micky could hardly believe his luck. Ingram, fabled director of *The Four Horsemen of the Apocalypse* starring Rudolph Valentino, had left Hollywood to escape interference from MGM's detested Louis B. Mayer, setting up his own Victorine Studios at Nice.

Taken under the wing of Harry Lachman, an accomplished painter working for Ingram as stills photographer, Powell's first job in movies consisted of sweeping floors between takes of *Mare Nostrum* and carrying props. He eagerly took this golden opportunity to observe a crack Hollywood film unit at close quarters, learning the trade literally from the ground upwards.

During the course of the production, and despite catastrophes such as dropping a valuable batch of glass negatives – 'I was the strange cultured young Englishman who had a remarkable gift for falling over and dropping things', Powell told Kevin Gough Yates many years later – he graduated to assistant stills photographer and, eventually, title designer. When the holiday ended, Micky had no thought of ever returning to the National Provincial Bank.

Ingram's next feature, a 'horror' story based on Somerset Maugham's *The Magician*, even included a brief but unbilled appearance by Powell, recalled in his autobiography. '[Rex Ingram] suddenly announced... that I was to be included as a comedy relief... I was clapped into a make-up chair, covered in Leichner make-up, had my head shaved, was allotted a battered suit of clothes, a pair of glassless spectacles, a toy balloon, and a bag of bananas... and was told to be funny. I tried'.

The Garden of Allah followed, with another minor appearance by Micky Powell, this time receiving his first screen credit as 'Tourist'. 'I never saw a final cut on *The Garden of Allah* until... early in 1928 at the Tivoli Cinema in the Strand in London', he later wrote. 'I went to see if I were still in the picture, whether my name was still on the credits. I was. It was'.

Although considered by many to be the best of three filmed versions of the story, *The Garden of Allah*'s mixed reception led to Ingram's enforced return to Hollywood. Powell remained in France where Lachman, impressed by Micky's comic turns, devised a series of two reel comedies called *Travelaughs* with Micky as star. Long thought to be 'lost', in the mid-1980s several of these films were discovered to have survived and were restored by the National Film Archive. 'The scheme was to fill a coach with tourists', Powell recalled. 'Run them round the Riviera and involve them in adventures and ecapades'. Along the way he also gained his first brief experience as director.

Harry sent me out to 'get some shots of hill-towns, and don't waste any film'. I worked out a series of dissolves in the camera, which gave an impression of Carros in about twenty seconds. Harry was astonished. He looked at me with new respect. 'Powell! That wasn't bad', he said.

Michael Powell finally returned to England in 1928 with Lachman, who had landed a job at British International Pictures' new studios at Elstree. Beginning as Reader in the Story Department, Micky learned of Alfred Hitchcock's reluctance to allow photographers on to the set of his latest film, *Champagne*. Boldly announcing that he would take the stills himself – which he promptly did – Powell astutely attached himself to the Hitchcock unit, again working as stills photographer on *The Manxman*, before being invited by the director to contribute ideas on his next movie, *Blackmail*.

● **20-year-old Michael Powell, embarking on a career in the movies.**

The sensational success of *The Jazz Singer* in America in October 1927 had signalled the end of the 'silent' era, but it was to be a full two years before *Blackmail* became 'Britain's First Talking Picture'; even then Hitchcock worked largely without British International's knowledge.

Uncredited on all versions, Powell claimed a screenwriting involvement with the silent release of the film after suggesting the British Museum as the location for the closing reel chase (which was also in the sound version). Either the company was unable to gain permission to film there or, as Hitchcock later told François Truffaut, there was not enough light inside the museum, so a combination of sets and process photography was used to create the effect. Powell was not otherwise involved with the production and at the time of shooting was again in France visiting his father. When he returned to Britain, he was approached by Jerry Jackson, an American lawyer turned distributor working for United Artists. Ideal Films, British distributors of *Travelaughs,* had hired Jackson to produce *Caste,* and he in turn hired Powell as screenwriter although Micky later claimed that he co-directed much of the film in the absence of credited director Campbell Gullan. This led to a further script assignment on *77 Park Lane,* a full-scale feature filmed simultaneously with three different casts for English, Spanish and French release versions. It was here that Michael Powell met the actor who would feature in more of his productions than anyone else:

a sulky, handsome young man with a mane of black hair and magnetic eyes, almost too romantically handsome to be true. Then one day I saw him giggling with one of the sound engineers and I realised that it was all a pose and he had a sense of humour... His name was Esmond Knight.

For his final screenwriting-only assignment, Micky collaborated with Miles Malleson on the independent Gloria Swanson production *A Perfect Understanding*, co-starring Laurence Olivier, but found himself also taking on duties as second unit director:

I very soon got fired, for there were inadequate instructions and then no money given to the second unit... I was asked to create Antibes with a concrete landing place, a cushion, a speedboat and Portsmouth harbour. It wasn't successful.

Partly through his association with Hitchcock and strongly supported by the persuasive Jerry Jackson, Michael was now approached by distributors Ideal Films to direct their next available 'quota quickie'.

With home film production accounting for less than five per cent of movies shown on British screens, Parliament passed the 1927 Cinematograph Films Act, forcing cinemas and renters to include a fixed 'quota' of British-made features in their programme, rising to 20 per cent by 1936. Any film carrying a 'quota ticket' was guaranteed a circuit booking. Established studios such as Gaumont-British, Gainsborough and British International continued to make genuine British

● Michael Powell's first feature *Two Crowded Hours* – 'A thrilling comedy drama of crime and detection'. Jerry Verno (centre) and John Longden (right) look suitably astounded.

features, while a vast number of small independent film producers – almost 400 new companies were registered between 1930 and 1935 – provided cheaply-made second features of variable quality which nevertheless were assured a release simply by virtue of being British. Hollywood studios now opened production units in England – Warner Brothers at Teddington, Fox at Wembley and Paramount at Elstree – employing local talent to produce ostensibly 'British' films, many of which had been previously rejected by the story departments of the parent company in America. These inexpensive and quickly-made pictures were the true 'quota quickies', produced by the Hollywood giants simply as a means of maintaining their domination of British screens.

Producers wanted 'quickies' made as cheaply as possible and such economies did not come easily. It was a mark of a director's ingenuity to come up with a film as inexpensively as possible while maintaining a semblance of quality on the screen. Powell was one of many directors, technicians and actors who got their real start in movies in these low-budget support features: between 1931 and 1936 he directed 23 movies for various companies, even – with Jerry Jackson – producing three films under their own banner, Westminster Films. Mostly, however, the duo worked for the British units of Warner Brothers or Fox, Michael Balcon's Gaumont-British, and finally the Joe Rock Studios, who produced *The Man Behind The Mask* in 1936.

Many personnel involved with 'quickies' later disappeared from the industry, as did some companies and even the films themselves. At the time of writing, 12 of Powell's films of this period are classed officially 'lost', although given the finding of 10 previously missing items between 1986 and 1990 in the Pinewood vaults and the British Film Institute's continuing programme of research, their rediscovery cannot be discounted.

1931

Two Crowded Hours Michael Powell's first feature as director, *Two Crowded Hours* was produced by Jerry Jackson for the Film Engineering Company and distributed by the British arm of Fox Pictures. With accomplished players John Longden (star of *Blackmail)* and cockney character actor Jerry Verno, shooting was completed in 12 days in April 1931 in and around London's Soho. 'It was played for laughs and thrills', Powell said, 'and we were paid £1 per foot by Fox. We got £4,000 on delivery so obviously we had to make it for £3,000'. Although a few stills survive, there is no known print of *Two Crowded Hours* in existence.

My Friend the King Actually Powell's third film as director, *My Friend the King* – another comedy starring Jerry Verno – was finished and on release while editing took place on the just-completed *Rynox*. The unlikely plot concerning a kidnapped Ruritanian prince and a London taxi driver ran a predictable course. During his first year as a feature director, Powell worked on five pictures. 'They couldn't all... be good and they weren't', he later wrote, considering this 'a very weak story... I only remember it as a complete failure'.

Rynox Within a week of completing *Two Crowded Hours*, Michael Powell began shooting on *Rynox*; 'not a quota-quickie production. It was a British feature, financed and distributed by Ideal Films, a respectable British film-maker'. Further improvements included a slightly larger budget – 'I think we got paid £4,500 for it' – and a stronger storyline with a screenplay by Philip Macdonald, Powell and Jackson from Macdonald's rather convoluted novel. Forty years later, Micky Powell hailed Philip Macdonald as 'the best thriller writer in those days and he still is, as far as I am concerned, one of the best'. Long considered lost, a print of *Rynox* was discovered in 1990 after 50 years languishing in the vaults at Pinewood Studios, acquired by the National Film Archive and transferred on to safety film – the earliest surviving example of Powell's work as a feature director.

Rynox brought Powell his first serious notice from film critics, with C.A. Lejeune of *The Observer* enthusiastically pronouncing that there were only three worthwhile directors in England: Hitchcock, Anthony Asquith and Michael Powell; this at a time when Hitchcock and Asquith had made 23 films between them compared with Powell's two modest efforts.

The Rasp Despite similar credentials to *Rynox*, *The Rasp* – a murder thriller from another Philip Macdonald story – 'refused to become a film and remained a book', according to Powell, although 'by this time [Macdonald]... became interested in us and volunteered to write two or three original scripts for us'. The 'Rasp' of the title refers to the file-like tool of that name which is the murder weapon in the story.

● *C.O.D.* is still one of Powell's lost films of the early 1930s. We may never know what Garry Marsh is up to.

The Star Reporter Powell later recalled *The Star Reporter* as 'fun and I was not ashamed of it. Harold French was a real pro. He understood comedy timing and I learned from him every day'. This now 'lost' film was released as support to Frank Capra's *Platinum Blonde*. 'It scarcely has the sparkle of the big feature', said one review, at which Powell 'was delighted. Never had such praise'. Economy was paramount in making 'quickies'. Powell 'said to Jerry [Jackson], "Give me a hand camera", so he said "You realise they're £8 to hire". I said 'I don't want to haggle, I want to go down to Southampton and shoot some stuff of the *Queen Mary*"... I went down and shot some very good stuff of the liner coming in and docking... very good quality and they just cut it into the picture.'

1932

Hotel Splendide *Hotel Splendide* was the first of Powell's films for Gaumont-British who had recently invited Michael Balcon to take charge of production at their Lime Grove Studios in Shepherd's Bush. Balcon later produced such classics for Gaumont as *The 39 Steps* and *Rome Express* before taking command at Ealing Studios. *Hotel Splendide* was another vehicle for Jerry Verno who here fell into the tradition of comedy thriller heroes whose screen characters invariable use their own real first name – later examples of this include George Formby and Norman Wisdom – in an effort to establish some sort of screen 'identity'. A print of *Hotel*

Splendide was recovered from the Pinewood Studio vaults at the beginning of 1990 and restored by the National Film Archive.

C.O.D. *C.O.D.* was the first picture made by Westminster Films, the company formed by Michael Powell and producer Jerry Jackson. The opening logo, showing Big Ben, anticipated Alexander Korda's use of the same landmark for his London Films a few years later, by which time Westminster Films had folded. *C.O.D.* – featuring Garry Marsh in a rare leading role as a hapless down and out – has apparently failed to survive. Critics of the day did, however, consider the direction of Michael Powell to be 'brilliant'.

His Lordship The second Westminster Films production, *His Lordship* was Jerry Verno's fourth film for Powell, and his last appearance for the director until *The Red Shoes* 16 years later. A 1936 British film of the same title starring George Arliss has no connection with Powell's *His Lordship*, a musical comedy considered 'broad' by reviewers, which again is considered officially 'lost'.

Born Lucky Powell here directed a fifth conscutive screenplay by Ralph Smart, who was later to turn to directing but achieved his greatest successes in television during the 1960s as producer / director of *The Adventures of Robin Hood, Danger Man* and *The Invisible Man. Born Lucky* again featured John Longden in a major role with René Ray as the romantic interest. Powell recalled this final Westminster production as 'real schmaltz':

Jerry Jackson… got me into [it]… Talbot O'Farrell, who at that time was a big headliner, sort of Irish balladmonger, and a little girl who was too obviously the broken flower. It was notable for one thing; it was art directed by Ian Campbell-Gray, and he would have made a great name for himself but he was killed in the war.

1933

The Fire Raisers With nine releases in the previous two years, Powell surprisingly made only one film during 1933. *The Fire Raisers* was the first production in a four-picture deal between Powell/Jackson and Gaumont-British. Not a 'quota quickie', *The Fire Raisers*, at Powell's estimation, cost around £12,000 to produce and featured a much stronger cast than the director had previously had at his command led by West End star Leslie Banks, just back from a starring role in RKO's *The Most Dangerous Game (Hounds of Zaroff)* in Hollywood. 'It was the first time that I had worked with a great actor', Powell later wrote.

An original screenplay, described by Powell as 'a sort of Warner Brothers Newspaper Headline Story', *The Fire Raisers* was the most successful of the director's films to that date, attracting considerable and favourable attention from critics; *The Observer* remarking that 'Michael Powell has economical ideas on continuity that save his producers hundreds of pounds a week', although they felt he had 'yet to prove he can think big'. 'I still believe that Michael Powell might make a

● The great Leslie Banks as David Barr, master shipbuilder in *Red Ensign*, a realistic and well received shipyard drama of 1934.

good picture', the review continued, 'but not so long as he is regarded as the champion "quickie" merchant of the industry'. A nitrate print of *The Fire Raisers* was among those films rescued from the Pinewood Studio vaults in early 1990.

Michael Powell made his first contact here with Film Editor Derek Twist and Art Director Alfred Junge, both of whose work was to feature significantly in his future career. Junge had just completed *Jew Süss* for Gaumont-British starring Conrad Veidt and featuring Frank Cellier and Francis L. Sullivan, both of whom appeared in *The Fire Raisers*.

1934

The Night of the Party Powell reluctantly accepted *Night of the Party* from Michael Balcon as an already complete script called *Murder Party*, convinced that he had been tricked into making the picture after Balcon claimed that the studio was standing idle. With the pick of any of the actors on a Gaumont-British contract list including Leslie Banks, Ian Hunter and Ernest Thesiger, Powell recalled 'It was one of those stories, where everybody's a character and it ends up with an Old Bailey court case with all the wrong people. I was bored to death with it but I did the best I could'. The film remained unreleased while Powell worked on *The Fire Raisers* and 'became a friend of Leslie Banks. We went back to *Night of the Party* and did three days extra retakes on it which made a little more sense of it'. Missing for over 50 years, a copy of *Night of the Party* was discovered at Pinewood in early 1990 and deposited with the NFA, whose new print was seen for the first time at the 1990 London Film Festival.

Red Ensign A third film in quick succession starring Leslie Banks, again with an original screenplay by Powell and Jackson based on a newspaper article, *Red Ensign* was more fondly recalled by Powell than many of his works of this period. Set in a Clyde shipyard, Powell surrounded his star with authentic Scottish actors and proudly boasted of 'the elaborate staging of the shipyard, the big, sweeping exteriors [filmed on location in Glasgow], the high standard of the performances and the sincerity of the actors, the overall seriousness of my approach to directing our story', the effect of which was that 'people just didn't know what to make of [it].'

Released on home video in 1992, *Red Ensign* was loosely remade by British National in 1943 as *The Shipbuilders*, directed by John Baxter and starring Clive Brook.

Something Always Happens Despite being a return to quota pictures at Warner Brothers' new Teddington Studios, Powell nevertheless considered *Something Always Happens* 'a very good comedy. We played it all out for laughs and great speed, excellent dialogue. It was about a chap [Ian Hunter] who never paid for anything... Ian was a very good comedian'. Reviews were surprisingly good for this 69-minute picture which contained all of the ingredients which made many 'quickies' attractive to audiences. The performances of Ian Hunter, Nancy O'Neill and Peter Gawthorne were highly praised, as was Michael Powell's 'imaginative' direction.

The Girl in the Crowd *The Girl in the Crowd* was another 'lost' Warner Brothers quota picture which Powell claimed was 'forced' on him. 'They were American B-pictures without the slickness and confidence that genuine American B's have got', he said later. A cast less polished than in his more recent films nevertheless yielded a new British actress and future star. 'I always say that Michael Powell really was the man who started my career', recalls Googie Withers. 'I was seventeen, and I'd never even done a play'.

Dancing in the chorus of a West End revue, she was spotted by a Warner Brothers casting director and 'went down to do a test at the Riverside Studios – I knew nothing about making films'. First impressions were not encouraging.

The girl who was playing second lead burst into tears and [Michael Powell] sacked her – on the set on the first day of shooting. He turned to me and said 'Who are you?' I was stammering and shaking in my boots by this time, and he said 'Well get up and do this scene'. I looked at him in horror and said 'I don't know it'. He said 'You've been watching it for two hours – if you don't know it by now you'll never make an actress'. So I got up and did it! That was the very first time I'd ever walked into a film studio or acted and I was immediately playing the leading part!

1935

Lazybones A slight and slow moving comedy which has dated badly, *Lazybones* was made at Twickenham Studios with, as Powell recalled, 'two West End artists [Ian Hunter and Claire Luce] who only came down after the show, and we shot all night. Can you imagine? Actors are resilient but it bloody well nearly killed me!' The film clearly betrays its stage origins, with *Monthly Film Bulletin* noting 'a very English background of old Manors, retainers, dogs and much talk of beer... Such an incredible story needs more pace and a lighter touch throughout'.

The Love Test Made for Fox-British at Wembley Studios, *The Love Test* is a lightweight but enjoyable romantic comedy with several notable features. Star Louis Hayward was soon bound for Hollywood and a starring career in swashbucklers like *The Man in the Iron Mask* and *Son of Monte Cristo*. 'He was a business man really and did very well in Hollywood', said Powell, who also claimed *The Love Test* as 'the first appearance of Bernard Miles in films or anywhere else for that matter'. Googie Withers featured as a flirtatious secretary ('Brings sunshine into dull lives, makes the bald grow hair!') in her second film for Powell, while the handling of a sequence showing the 'glamorizing' of the attractive Judy Gunn by her sophisticated neighbour Kathleen (Eve Turner) can be seen as a forerunner to the erotic transformation of Sister Ruth in *Black Narcissus* 12 years later. Another of Powell's films rediscovered in the late 1980s, *The Love Test* was screened at the 1990 London Film Festival.

The Phantom Light Completing the Gaumont-British deal, *The Phantom Light* was by far Michael Powell's most accomplished picture to date. Well photographed by Roy Kellino – later a director himself – and sharply edited by Derek Twist, the film also benefited greatly from an expert comic performance by Gordon Harker, a great character of British cinema described by Powell as 'wonderful in silent films, but even better in talkies. Close-ups were made for him, and we both took full advantage of it'.

For the role of Jim Pearce, Powell had wanted to cast Roger Livesey, then at the Old Vic in a company which included Charles Laughton and James Mason. After shooting a test of the actor, Powell was overruled by Michael Balcon who announced that he did not like Livesey's voice, which Powell considered one of his most attractive features! The role fell to the Gaumont contract player Ian Hunter.

Location work was much praised by critics. Although the film was set in Wales, Powell found a suitable spot in North Devon.

I went down to Hartland Point and right out to the Eddystone in the relief boat and one or two other lighthouses just to get different ideas. Some wonderful shots were shot at Hartland Point.

Of the film itself, Powell later enthused, 'I said "yes" to this one right away, and never regretted it. I enjoyed every minute'. So, too, did audiences.

● Gordon Harker as heroic, dashing lighthouse keeper Sam Higgins in *The Phantom Light* – 'There's two in the service handsomer than me'.

The Price of a Song After the full-scale British feature *The Phantom Light*, *The Price of a Song* was again a return to a modest thriller, though one with a more intelligent screenplay than most – which turned out to be the film's downfall. 'When a thriller's too ingenious it becomes a little picture', he said later. 'When it's simple it's got a chance of being big... It was a beautifully worked out thriller, almost Henry Jamesian... but in quota quickie terms'. *The Price of a Song* is a murder mystery of the type Columbo would solve on television some 40 years later by means of an apparently insignificant string of clues.

Sadly, this intriguing little picture is another 'missing' item in the Powell catalogue. Campbell Gullan, credited director of *Caste*, was star of the film, which also featured Felix Aylmer in an early supporting role.

Someday This well-received romance provided Margaret Lockwood with one of her earliest leading screen roles at the age of 19. She went on to become Britain's most popular film star of the 1940s in films like *The Man in Grey, The Wicked Lady* and *Love Story*. *Someday* brought Michael Powell into contact with Esmond Knight once more and was another of the director's films for Warner Brothers at their Teddington Studios.

1936

Her Last Affaire Powell was less happy about *Her Last Affaire,* 'a social comedy on a very old theme', made at Beaconsfield Studios, but was pleased to be working with Hugh Williams. On screen since 1931, Williams had been an impressive

● Rare shot of Powell with stars Hugh Williams and Viola Keats on the set of *Her Last Affaire* – one of several 'lost' films rediscovered at Pinewood during the late 1980s.

Steerforth in MGM's *David Copperfield* (1935), but had immediately returned to England, seemingly unimpressed by Hollywood. A later sojourn took him back across the Atlantic to play the dissolute Hindley Earnshaw of Emily Brontë's *Wuthering Heights* for Samuel Goldwyn in 1939, but his best work was to be seen in British pictures like *Rome Express* (1932), *Brief Ecstasy* and *Bank Holiday* (both 1937). Powell found him to be 'an extremely polished, arrogant young actor'.

The original stage play of *Her Last Affaire* had been a great success, with Gracie Fields taking her first straight role. Googie Withers took the part in the film which was not well received on release although Powell claimed 'We worked very hard on it'. A rogue print of *Her Last Affaire* with a cast drawn largely from the West End stage was discovered in the mid-1980s and restored by the National Film Archive.

The Brown Wallet Michael Powell later claimed to have been talked into many of his films for Warners – of which this was another – either by Jerry Jackson or Irving Asher, production head of the British studio. *The Brown Wallet*, from Stacy Aumonier's crime story, was reviewed as a 'good story with a twist in it. Some accomplished acting. An easy support feature' and featured an early screenplay by Ian Dalrymple, later a successful writer/producer in the 1940s.

Crown v Stevens Following his roles in *The Brown Wallet* and now, *Crown v Stevens*, star Patric Knowles was soon to follow the same route out to Hollywood as that taken by Errol Flynn, who had been recommended to Jack Warner by Irving Asher after making one British quota picture, *Murder in Monte Carlo* (1935). Fulfilling one of the 'indirect' aims of the British film units of the major American companies, Asher now 'discovered' Knowles and later Ian Hunter, both of whom would appear with Flynn in Warner Brothers' Hollywood production of *The Adventures of Robin Hood* in 1938.

Crown v Stevens, meanwhile, gave smaller roles to Googie Withers and Glennis Lorrimer, whose chief claim to fame was as 'The Gainsborough Lady' in the opening logo of that studio's films. Powell recalled Beatrix Thomson – the heroine/bad girl of the story – as 'a very good actress' who was 'fantastically good in this, but that was all it had'.

The Man Behind the Mask A feature, as opposed to another 'quickie', *The Man Behind the Mask* was made by Joe Rock, an American who had been involved in vaudeville before taking a stab at Hollywood where he produced a string of two reelers starring Stan Laurel in the days before he met Oliver Hardy. Now settled in Britain, Rock 'believed in the off-beat picture'.

The Man Behind the Mask was 'a very old-fashioned thriller', said Powell. 'It was actually a story published in magazine form of four or five episodes rather after the style of A.E.W. Mason detective thrillers'. Finding the material unpromising, the director 'did my best to make it into a really rather sort of a German-type expressionist thriller. It was very hard work indeed because we had no money...The only good that came out of it was that I met Joe Rock'.

Michael Powell's final work before embarking on his career as a major feature director, *The Man Behind the Mask* was made by a small independent company and is officially considered lost.

In 1971, with few of these films available for viewing and little chance of being contradicted, Powell was quick to dismiss the work of those years as of little merit. Googie Withers featured in five 'quickies', and firmly believes they were not as bad as he suggests. 'People loved them', she says, 'and they still talk about them today'. Of the quality of the films themselves: 'They were very good – a lot of them were excellent. One took short cuts of course and you did an awful lot of work in a short time. But I would never have been where I am today without the "quickies" because that's where I learned my trade'.

Powell's disaffection for this period stems from his work on *77 Park Lane*, a comparatively big budget (£8,000) film. By next agreeing to make 'quickies' – with production costs often set at less than half that figure – he now felt himself to be working in a much smaller league. Nevertheless, those years provided valuable experience both for the director and the actors – many drawn from the West End stage, as Googie Withers recalls. 'We were all starting our careers and there were a lot of extremely well known actors in them, not just beginners like myself'. Among those who worked for Powell at this time were future stars Margaret Lockwood, Leslie Banks, Ian Hunter, Esmond Knight, John Laurie, Bernard Miles, Patric Knowles, Louis Hayward and Hugh Williams. Micky Powell, however, greeted the news in 1986 that a handful of 'lost' films had in fact survived with mock horror: 'My reputation can't stand any more rediscoveries!'

2

The edge and back

In 1930, Powell had spotted a short item in *The Observer* concerning the forced evacuation of St Kilda in the Hebrides. Fashioning a story around the piece would show the difficulties involved in the upheaval of leaving the only home the islanders had ever known, but it was not until 1936 that he found a sympathetic ear for the proposed film.

A book could be written on the making of *The Edge of the World*, and that is precisely what Michael Powell did in 1937 when Faber and Faber published his account as *20,000 Feet on Foula* the cryptic title referring to the amount of film exposed during shooting on the island (the book was reissued in 1990 as *Edge of the World*).

During shooting of *The Man in the Mask,* he persuaded Joe Rock not only to finance the new project but to shoot it on the island location itself – 40 miles off the coast of western Scotland in the raging Atlantic. With a £20,000 budget, the cast and crew were assembled, the former featuring a mix of experienced actors such as John Laurie and Finlay Currie – to the young cast and crew awe-inspiringly rumoured to be over 60 years old (he was 58) – and newer faces including Niall MacGinnis, two years after his debut in *Turn of the Tide,* the first film financed by J. Arthur Rank.

The production met its first obstacle with the refusal of the owners of St Kilda to allow filming. Since evacuation, the island had become an important bird sanctuary, not to be disrupted for the sake of a mere motion picture. Miraculously, with the help of local authority John Mathieson, a topographically-similar island was found 200 miles further north in the Shetlands. If anything even more ferocious than St Kilda in situation, Foula was nevertheless still inhabited which, it was hoped, would ease some of the likely problems for the company during filming.

Five months were spent on Foula, with a rough 'village' of primitive wooden huts constructed for the 'comfort' of the film unit. Belle Chrystall and Frankie Reidy (later Mrs Michael Powell) were allocated more comfort-able accommodation, while others preferred to sleep on board the company's steamer rather than brave conditions in the huts on the ferociously cold nights.

The people of Foula thankfully accepted the presence of the film crew, with virtually all appearing in the finished picture. Evidently Powell and his men avoided those problems experienced by the Ealing production *Whisky Galore* (1949) on Barra in the Outer Hebrides when a cameraman innocently asked one inhabitant for permission to 'shoot' (film) his mother. That crew was regarded with deep suspicion from then on!

● Powell's first major feature, *The Edge of the World* with Belle Chrystall and Niall MacGinnis.

Contact with the mainland was lost soon after the unit arrived in mid-June 1936. The one scheduled trip per week to purchase supplies, collect rushes and send exposed reels to the lab often could not be made due to bad weather and it was not unusual for the company to be completely isolated for weeks at a time. The weather also quickly put the film behind schedule and in mid-October the national press reported the company marooned without a radio, perilous seas preventing their escape. Joe Rock decreed that as soon as was safe, the unit itself should be evacuated. Unaware of the headlines, Powell and his team were finally lifted from Foula after 11 days of continuous storms and, on returning to Lerwick, managed to steal a few necessary key shots on their final morning before disbanding.

For the mammoth job of condensing almost four hours of footage to a manageable length, Powell requested the services of Derek Twist, film editor on *Red Ensign* and *The Phantom Light*. 'The Edge of the World* was entirely saved for me by Derek Twist', said Powell later. 'An editor with the eye of a hawk, the memory of an Indian and a heart of granite… [who] will never get a quarter of the credit which is due to him'.

Unanimously praised were the location settings, with spectacular scenery impressively photographed by three credited cameramen. The inexperienced Monty Berman (later producer of television's *The Saint, Randall and Hopkirk* and *The Champions*) had been with the unit when they landed on Foula, but found himself replaced by old hand Ernest Palmer – just, according to Powell, as Berman was hitting his stride. Skeets Kelly handled most of the mainland shots and the documentary-style sequences on board the trawler. The beauty of the island and the mystical aspects of the story were well captured, with the many striking images including the ghostly appearance of the former islanders and Peter Manson's memories of his soon-to-be-deserted home. Particularly moving was Robbie Manson's funeral procession, as a melancholy mist enshrouded both the mourners and the weeping island itself.

Released in September 1937, *The Edge of the World* gained mostly favourable reviews. *Variety* called it 'a minor film of little interest', although Joe Rock astutely arranged a US distribution deal for the picture which was then voted one of the best Foreign Films of the year by the New York critics. British reviewers were considerably more enthusiastic with favourable comparision being made with the work of Robert Flaherty, celebrated documentary film-maker of *Nanook of the North* and *Man of Aran*. *Motion Picture Herald* advised 'it is emphatically a picture the exhibitor should view for himself, for it falls into no recognized category'. A 62 minute 1940 reissue was for many years the only version of the film available, and was incorporated into the 1978 *Return to the Edge of the World*. The National Film Archive in 1990 produced a new print running at 80 minutes, shown at the London Film Festival and released on home video.

For Michael Powell, *The Edge of the World* was a great personal triumph. After five years in 'quota quickies', this first major project had been carried through largely by stubbornness and a determination to see it completed. '[It] was a turning point of my life in art, and I found it impossible to return to the world of cheap thrillers'.

In late 1930s European cinema, success often brought with it a first class ticket to Hollywood. Many actors, including Ronald Colman, George Sanders and Charles Laughton, sailed to America never to return. Directors, too, migrated from various parts of Europe. Germany's Fritz Lang and France's Jean Renoir would soon be joined by Alfred Hitchcock from England as top American studio directors. With good notices in America Michael Powell was seemingly also bound for Hollywood, but before he began that long, probably one-way voyage, he met Alexander Korda.

Korda's career had taken him from his native Hungary and a spell in journalism to film-making in America, France and finally England where, in 1933 at Denham, he set up London Films, surrounded by as many Hungarians as he could find including his brothers Zoltan and Vincent. 1934's *The Private Life of Henry VIII*, directed by Korda, had become the first British film to win an Academy Award (Charles Laughton, Best Actor) and there followed the quality productions *Rembrandt, The Four Feathers* and *Things to Come* with an impressive roster of stars including Robert Donat, Laurence Olivier, Vivien Leigh, Merle Oberon and Ralph Richardson. Denham now became home for Powell, whose first assignment was as director of a one-minute tea commercial featuring Ralph Richardson and Flora Robson, perhaps his least distinguished cinematic achievement. Next was to be *Burmese Silver,* a vehicle for Conrad Veidt and Sabu. Powell was sent to scout locations in Burma, only to be informed upon his return that the film had

● 'Michael Powell at home prior to flying out to scout locations for *Burmese Silver* starring Sabu and Conrad Veidt'. The film was never made. Powell's two dogs, Eric and Spangle, seen in this 1937 shot, later became film stars of a sort, appearing in *Contraband*, *A Matter of Life and Death* and *Colonel Blimp*.

been shelved and that he was to direct Veidt in *The Spy in Black*.

At a first script conference for *The Spy in Black* – Michael had found the initial draft completely unworkable – Korda engineered a first introduction between Powell and yet another of those Hungarians who populated Denham.

Born on 5 December 1902 at Miskolc, northern Hungary and educated at Prague and Stuttgart, Imrie Pressburger had abandoned a likely career in civil engineering following the death of his father. In Berlin in 1928 he entered the world of journalism as 'Emmerich Pressburger' and two years later was a contract writer at leading German film studio, UFA. With the rise to power of Hitler's Nazi party, he moved first to Paris and then in 1935 to Britain where he was immediately signed to London Films – at that time virtually a refuge for Hungarian emigrés.

A co-credit on *The Challenge* (1938) followed a couple of unproduced screenplays before Korda offered him the rewrite of *The Spy in Black*. 'I took it away and read it and re-read it until I came up with the idea to make a smaller part into a larger part', Pressburger later told Kevin Gough-Yates. 'So… I was sitting waiting to be called into Korda's office whilst in another corner sat all these voluminous chaps… talking about me… I hadn't met Michael before'.

According to Powell, Pressburger 'produced a very small piece of rolled-up paper, and addressed the meeting' while he 'listened, spellbound'. The newcomer had created new characters, changed plots and, in the director's words, 'turned the story on its head. I glanced across the table at Irving [Asher, producer] and his unfortunate screenwriter: they were sitting with their mouths open…'.

'I had always dreamt of this phenomenon', Powell wrote, 'a screenwriter with the heart and mind of a novelist, who would be interested in the medium of film, and who would have wonderful ideas, which I would turn into even more wonderful images, and who only used dialogue to clarify the plot'.

Powell was equally thrilled to be working with Conrad Veidt – 'one of the greatest names in European cinema and one of the most romantic and magnetic men alive'. After a screen career in Germany including *Waxworks* and *The Cabinet of Doctor Caligari,* Veidt had been in England since 1935 with box-office successes including *Rome Express, I Was a Spy* and *The Passing of the Third Floor Back* behind him.

Powell and Pressburger both agreed with Korda that Veidt had not yet revealed his true potential in British films. Regular meetings between director, writer and both leading players led to a finished screenplay constructed to give Conrad Veidt ample opportunity to display his dramatic talents as well as a rarely-seen comic ability.

Set during the First World War, the story was filmed in the Orkneys, about 80 miles from Foula, scene of *The Edge of the World*, and was released a month before the Second World War was declared, to great critical and box-office acclaim. This was helped by an uncanny coincidence when a German submarine entered Scapa Flow and torpedoed a British battleship. For Michael Powell, not only had he progressed to the backing of a major studio and directed another successful picture, he had made the most important acquaintance of his professional life in Emeric Pressburger – 'a little mouse-like character' – with whom he would form one of the most remarkable partnerships in British cinema history. 'I had seen a marvel: a screenwriter who could really write. I was not going to let him get away in a hurry'.

But first, Powell was to be involved briefly in helping his friend Vernon Sewell,

● Conrad Veidt copes with wartime shortages and restrictions in *The Spy in Black* – lucky he brought his motorbike!

Production Assistant on *The Edge of the World*, with the screenplay of a short film adapted from Tolstoy. Directed by Sewell, *What Men Live By* is a rare curiosity featuring Esmond Knight which was released in 1939.

That same year, Alexander Korda set in motion his most extravagant production to date. *The Thief of Bagdad* was a lavish Technicolor remake of the story previously filmed in 1924 by Douglas Fairbanks. Influenced by Warner Brothers' 1935 *A Midsummer Night's Dream* – originally to have been directed by acclaimed theatre director Max Reinhardt – Korda announced that *The Thief of Bagdad* would be directed by German theatre director Doctor Ludwig Berger who had just completed a screen version of *Cinderella*. However, as with the Warners' experiment where Reinhardt was replaced by William Dieterle, Berger's control was soon undermined when Korda realized the style of film his director was making – exotic, subtle, artistic – while Alex and brother Vincent had planned an extravagant colour fantasy. On seeing the first sets, Alex urged 'Rebuild it four times as big and paint it pink!'

Even Berger's wish to use Strauss for the music of the film was opposed by Korda who wanted Miklos Rozsa to write the score. Rozsa was installed in a room next to Berger's office, working continuously on composing his themes, until Berger excitedly announced his 'discovery' of the genius in the next room! Rozsa's music, including the popular 'I Want To Be A Sailor', was a huge success, winning an Academy Award nomination and being among the first film scores to be released as a soundtrack album.

Michael Powell assumed increasingly greater responsibility as the unfortunate

Berger's active participation in the project dwindled. Tim Whelan was brought in to direct action scenes, while other sequences were directed by Art Director William Cameron Menzies (director of *Things to Come* and designer of *Gone with the Wind*) and Korda himself.

On 3 September war was declared with Germany, and Korda, a close friend of Winston Churchill, seized an opportunity already discussed with the future Prime Minister. Korda had convinced Churchill of cinema's potential as a propaganda tool, and promised to produce a film to that effect should conflict arise. During the First World War the British cinema industry had been virtually closed down for the duration and Korda had no intention of letting that happen again.

For *The Lion Has Wings,* Powell was assigned flying and combat scenes and accordingly set off to film whatever he could – at this stage there was no script – while other sections of the film were handled by Adrian Brunel and Brian Desmond Hurst. Ian Dalrymple retained overall control and set about organizing the production.

As Korda had promised, the film was shot, edited and on the screen within six weeks – an achievement which had the desired effect on Churchill, whose recommendation for the continued use of cinema for morale purposes was to become increasingly important. Inevitably, today the film – a shameless flag-waver featuring Ralph Richardson and Merle Oberon – contains much that is naïve and unconvincing, although at a time of war its message was met by more receptive ears. Powell's verdict: 'It was a hodgepodge'.

With British cinema's role throughout the coming conflict assured, Korda now transported his unfinished Arabian Nights fantasy to Hollywood, where he and his brother Zoltan completed *The Thief of Bagdad* at the United Artists studios. Many key personnel went over to the US to finish their work on the picture – Conrad Veidt, Sabu and Miklos Rozsa were among those who settled there – but Michael Powell was not involved in any of the American work on the film.

Finally released in both Britain and the US on Christmas Day 1940, *The Thief of Bagdad* was just the type of escapist film the public was ready for in wartime and proved a huge hit. At the 1941 Academy Awards it won Oscars for Vincent Korda (Colour Art Direction), Lawrence Butler and Jack Whitney (Special Effects) and Georges Périnal (Colour Cinematography), and became Korda's biggest grossing US release ever, although *Variety* found it 'stolid, slow and rather disjointed' with an 'unimpressive story and stagey acting' compared to the Fairbanks version which 'presented dash and movement to dominate the spectacular settings. Korda uses the reverse angle. As a result, audience interest is focused on the technical display'. Later versions of the story include a 1960 Italian production starring Steve Reeves and a British-French television remake (1978) with Roddy McDowell, Terence Stamp and Peter Ustinov in the roles played by Sabu, Conrad Veidt and Miles Malleson. With poor special effects and a charmless hero, this film completely failed to erase earlier productions from the memory.

The highly-praised colour – dictated by Vincent Korda's designs – had been a source of controversy between the unit and Dr Natalie Kalmus of the Technicolor company. At this time Kalmus and Technicolor retained almost total authority over the use of their trademark system. Micky Powell insisted that 'the genius over the whole thing… was Périnal… who had the most exquisite taste. You know, he and Vincent between them managed to make the colour some of the best that has ever been made – Périnal's close-ups – nobody has ever been able to light a human face up in the way that he does'. A firm favourite with audiences, a restored print of *The Thief of Bagdad* was premiered at the London Film Festival of November 1989, attended by Michael Powell.

Meanwhile, having completed his duties on *The Lion Has Wings*, Michael Powell eagerly teamed up with Emeric Pressburger again and decided to reunite the two stars of the successful *The Spy in Black*: Conrad Veidt, this time playing a Danish captain, and Valerie Hobson. By October 1939, *Contraband* was in production on the vacant Denham lot, financed by Lady Yule, the owner of Elstree Studios.

With the co-operation of the Admiralty, the Ministry of Economic Warfare, the Ministry of Information and an unnamed Contraband Control Port 'somewhere in England', shooting wrapped up in six weeks and included the first scenes to make use of the recently-enforced London blackout, which inspired the American release title of the film. This topicality guaranteed the film an appreciative audience when released the following April, and *Contraband* was a box-office hit.

Emeric Pressburger's script was scattered with moments of wit and the eccentricity which would mark the future works of The Archers, as when Conrad Veidt makes a getaway through a storeroom piled high with unsold plaster busts of Neville Chamberlain – an understated reference to the falling popularity of the British Prime Minister following the Munich episode.

One scene cut from the finished film featured 'an adorable little cigarette girl in another nightclub', said Powell. 'All lovely liquid eyes and nice long legs [in] a tiny scene with Conrad Veidt… Pity I didn't keep the clipping, because it was Deborah Kerr's first appearance on any screen'.

Michael now produced and photographed a much admired five-minute short of *An Airman's Letter to his Mother*, narrated by John Gielgud and based on an actual letter which had appeared in *The Times*. At about this time too the British government set up a Films Division within the Ministry of Information under National Gallery director Kenneth Clark, who thought his appointment 'an inexplicable choice… commonly attributed to the fact that… films were spoken of as "pictures", and I was believed to be an authority on pictures'. Although he 'had no qualifications for the job [and] knew nothing about the structure of the film world', Clark nevertheless brought great enthusiasm and, ultimately, expertise to the task of encouraging and in some cases sponsoring film production on approved subjects in order to aid the war effort. Powell and Pressburger were approached to tackle the subject of minesweeping, to which Powell replied

'That's First World War stuff. I want to make a film about Canada... being next to the USA, they will help to bring [them] in'.

Heading for the 49th Parallel, the border between Canada and North America, to scout locations, Pressburger came up with the plot of the film *en route,* and a starring cast was quickly contacted. Laurence Olivier, Leslie Howard, Anton Walbrook, Raymond Massey and Elisabeth Bergner all agreed to appear in the film at a basic minimum fee instead of their usual salaries, although Howard apparently later insisted on a percentage agreement, eventually met by Powell and Pressburger. The role of fanatical Nazi Lieutenant Hirth was to have been taken by Powell's friend Esmond Knight until the actor enlisted in the Navy. Instead, Hirth was played by Eric Portman, an experienced stage actor who had survived an improbable screen debut as 'Gypsy Carlos' in *Maria Marten, or the Murder in the Red Barn* with Tod Slaughter in 1935, and had made only four films over the next six years. Following his appearance in *49th Parallel,* Eric Portman was voted into second place behind Laurence Olivier in the *Picturegoer* Annual Awards, prompting the magazine to run an article entitled 'Who Is He?'

Courageously, Powell gave equal star billing to the composer of the film's majestic musical score, Ralph Vaughan Williams. One of the country's most revered composers, Vaughan Williams, at the age of 69, was working in the cinema for the first time at the suggestion of his friend, musical director Muir Mathieson. Williams provided a memorable score to the film and described the experience as 'the best lesson in composition I ever had'. He would later work on a number of other British films including *Scott of the Antarctic.*

For the first time on a major production, Powell was his own producer, and filming progressed as and when actors were available and weather conditions allowed. Raymond Massey had joined the Canadian army, so his scenes were shot at the Associated Sound News Studios in Montreal, while opening shots in Hudson Bay had to be caught before the ice appeared, and the Hutterite scenes were to coincide with the harvesting of the crop. Most other scenes could be put together at Denham, apart from those featuring the Nazi soldiers, which had to be filmed across the length and breadth of Canada. The sole 'casualty' of the production was Elisabeth Bergner, who 'defected' across the border to the United States instead of returning to London after filming her scenes in Canada. Glynis Johns replaced her, although most of the outdoor distance shots featuring Miss Bergner could still be used.

Echoing Googie Withers' experience on the set of *The Girl in the Crowd*, Robert Beatty witnessed an example of the director's sometimes harsh treatment of his actors during the making of *49th Parallel*. Although Beatty 'always got on well with Michael Powell and admired his professional expertise, I did find him on one occasion... a bit of a masochist'.

Filming with me was a young and inexperienced actor who delivered his lines badly. Instead of taking him aside, he shouted at him in front of the whole crew. After a few more takes the poor fellow became even more nervous and began drying his lines. Relentlessly

[Powell] went on... until the chap was reduced to a gibbering wreck... The scene was postponed to the following day and, as you may expect, another actor took over the part.

As if this were not enough, the scene was eventually left on the cutting room floor, deleting Beatty from the film altogether although he 'did dub the voice of an actual RCMP filmed on location at Alberta'. Of this unpleasant incident he recalled, 'I do feel that had Michael showed a little kindness and understanding, which Carol Reed had to a fantastic degree, the scene would not have had to be reshot and a great deal of footage would have been saved'.

With filming completed, David Lean was brought in as Film Editor, and cut the film to slightly over two hours with not a frame wasted. Frederick Young, Director of Cinematography on *49th Parallel*, was later to become David Lean's favourite cameraman, winning Academy Awards for his work on *Lawrence of Arabia*, *Doctor Zhivago* and *Ryan's Daughter*.

Released in November 1941, *49th Parallel* continued the run of successes for Powell and Pressburger – even more so when issued in the United States as *The Invaders* the following April. A huge success, it won Emeric Pressburger an Academy Award for Best Original Story and also received nominations for Best Screenplay and Best Film, losing to *Mrs Miniver*. Despite this mark of approval, there were some detractors who felt the German crewmen to be too sympathetically drawn, although the brutality of Hirth's character is clearly shown thoughout, even to the extent of executing one of his own men as a 'traitor'. 'This was one of the very first important films about the ideology of the Nazis', Pressburger recalled. 'We were fighting for our lives and for everything else. The Nazis were hateful sorts of fellows. Now all this has faded a bit [but] you only have to see the newsreels... But even among those Nazis we had a sympathetic sort of fellow'.

In January 1942, Powell defended *49th Parallel* to *The Times* who suggested that the film had 'not justified the time and money that were expended on its production', by pointing out that the picture had not yet been released in either Canada, the other Dominions or the United States, but had recouped its entire cost in England alone after only three months. This 'justifies the faith that the then Minister of Information placed in our venture', he continued, adding, 'It may also do much to hearten those gentlemen of the Select Committee of National Expenditure who, long before the film was completed and its results could possibly have been forseen by any but those closely concerned with the making of it, announced that they regarded "this kind of venture with the gravest misgivings"'. *49th Parallel* went on to be named as the top grossing film in the UK for 1941.

Michael later told *Sight and Sound*, 'From then on every film we made sprang organically from the one we'd just made because, first of all, we were guessing a year ahead what the general position of the war would be and what would be the propaganda message. After all, films take a year to make and get out... and so we had to be good guessers'.

3

A production of the Archers

With *49th Parallel* playing to capacity audiences, Powell and Pressburger were now approached by Rank to make a film for them, with the result that Micky 'said to Emeric that this phrase "one of our aircraft failed to return" was a wonderful one to build a story around and would he think about it'. Pressburger duly completed a plot outline, by which time the official phrase had become 'one of our aircraft is missing'. 'I guess they thought "failed to return" was too downbeat', said Powell. Rank, however, rejected the story-line, so Powell and Pressburger returned to *Contraband* backers Lady Yule and John Corfield who gladly accepted the new project.

The basic plot, a reversal of *49th Parallel*, this time telling of a British crew stranded in occupied enemy territory and their attempts to return home, was lifted (uncredited) by Warner Brothers for the following year's *Desperate Journey* starring Errol Flynn, Arthur Kennedy and Ronald Reagan.

Containing one of cinema's most spectacular opening sequences – an empty bomber crossing the night sky before exploding into an electricity pylon – *One of Our Aircraft is Missing* has very much of a documentary feel, helped considerably by Powell's decision not to feature any music, only natural sounds, and the absence of a major star name in the cast. Robert Helpmann, Pamela Brown and Joyce Redman all made their screen debuts in The Archers production, which also featured Googie Withers who had by now built a solid reputation in a number of films including four 'quickies' for Powell.

Until then I'd been doing mainly comedies, but [Powell] knew that I was half Dutch and that I spoke Dutch and German, so would be very useful in the part. He asked me, 'Do you think you can play it?' I said 'I could play it standing on my head,' and he said 'Well no-one thinks you can except for me. The producers say you are connected with George Formby comedies, and they want somebody they can believe in. I said, 'Well they'll believe in me, I can promise you'.

Miss Withers' performance was a personal triumph, and a turning point in her career. Critic C.A. Lejeune wrote that:

[she]… is a veteran of pictures, but she has never before had a part like this… She dresses like a man, in rough coat, overalls and boots. She wears no makeup, and pulls her hair up tight under a woollen scarf. I have seen [her] on the screen in ravishing gowns, fresh from the hands of the studio makeup department, but I have never known her to look better than she does here. There is character in every line of her face, and fire behind every word she speaks.

At the foot of the cast was 'Michael Powell... Despatching Officer', but far from this being an attempt to emulate Alfred Hitchcock's celebrated appearances in each of his films, Powell recalled merely that like everything else during wartime, actors were in short supply.

An embarassed Rank was forced to admit a definite error of judgement when *One of Our Aircraft is Missing*, released by British National in June 1942, met with great public and critical acclaim. Cut by about 20 minutes for US release, it became Powell and Pressburger's second consecutive picture to win a Best Screenplay nomination at the American Academy Awards – the only time in his career that Michael Powell would find his name put forward for an 'Oscar' – the film this time losing out to *Casablanca*.

It was during during the making of *One of Our Aircraft is Missing* that Powell and Pressburger took the logical step of forming their own independent company, The Archers. Future productions would carry the joint credit title: Written, Produced and Directed by Michael Powell and Emeric Pressburger.

Powell's agent Christopher Mann was aghast that he should concede so much screen credit to a 'mere' writer. The director, however, shrewdly recognized the enormous contribution which Emeric's ideas and scripts were to make to The Archers and was more than happy to acknowledge this. Future cameraman Christopher Challis recalls the precise role played by each in the partnership: 'Emeric very often got the ideas. Michael used to say that Emeric wrote the scripts and he translated them into English, which was a little unfair'. After a revision period, a finished shooting script would be produced, at which time 'Emeric took over the reins as producer. He fended off the Alex Kordas and the John Davises, taking all that awful front office business off Michael's shoulders while the film was being made. Emeric was much more diplomatic with those sort of people, whereas Michael would throw them off the set!'

For the next 15 years, Powell would not enter into any major film project without Pressburger at his side, and although Emeric would occasionally work on an 'outside' screenplay such as the 1946 *Wanted for Murder*, Christopher Challis confirms that 'They were incredibly loyal to each other. I couldn't think of two more unlikely people on surface values to form a partnership, but they were perfect foils for each other, and are the only two who I've never heard one say a bad thing about the other'.

For the first Archers venture solely as producers, Michael Powell's friend Vernon Sewell wrote and directed *The Silver Fleet* with Gordon Wellesley: a story inspired by the real-life hijacking of a U-Boat, seized and brought to England by a Dutch crew under order from a saboteur calling himself 'Piet Hein'. The Netherlands government gave every assistance, arranging Sewell's secondment to the Dutch Navy where he collected material on the sabotage of Nazi shipping. Powell took little active part in the project, which was super-

- 1930s studio portrait of favourite actor Esmond Knight, at a time when Powell 'spoke of him in the same breath as Laurence Olivier and Rex Harrison'.

vised by Pressburger and Associate Producer (and star) Ralph Richardson. Googie Withers confirmed her rising status as a dramatic actress in the film, but its most remarkable feature was the reappearance of Esmond Knight when most thought his career at an end. Persuaded – ironically by Vernon Sewell – to enlist with the Royal Navy in 1941, the actor had lost one eye and become blinded in the other when his ship *Prince of Wales* received a direct hit from the *Bismarck*. He was told that he would never see again, and a benefit evening held by his fellow actors suggested that he would never act again either. Later operations restored limited sight in his remaining eye, but at the time of *The Silver Fleet*, Esmond Knight was totally blind. Googie Withers explains, 'his wife Frances said "Don't be sorry and pitiful and all that. He's just been to this rehabilitation place where they make them laugh at the disability"'.

The problems encountered by a blind actor would seem to be insurmountable, but 'Frances would come down on the set and pace out what it was to walk from a door, and she would set that up in their home and rehearse him'. Similarly, the actor 'learned his lines by listening to them. [Frances] recorded them for him or she would say them over and over', says Miss Withers, who relates on a more personal level. 'I didn't realise until lunch how difficult it is for a blind person to eat. How does a man who can't see 'bone' a Dover Sole? Suddenly he put his fork into what was the tail and lifted up the whole thing - I burst out laughing and he said "Alright, what am I doing?"' This incident was put to use in a scene where von Schiffer is eating spaghetti; the apparently disgusting table manners illustrating the bestial nature of the Gestapo chief.

Many reviewers noted the performance. *Monthly Film Bulletin* wrote 'Special interest attaches to Esmond Knight's capable portrayal of the savage Gestapo chief… never once does he betray his disability', while *Motion Picture Herald* called it 'a truly remarkable triumph of personal character over physical circumstance'. Googie Withers fondly recalls Esmond Knight as 'a lovely, very funny man'.

Following the modest success of *The Silver Fleet*, Vernon Sewell went on to to direct a number of films for British National at the Elstree Studios.

The Archers' first full production which followed also proved their most controversial to date. There had been rumblings concerning Pressburger's storylines, with a sympathetic German character in *The Spy in Black* and the German crew in *49th Parallel* written as fully realized, resourceful and intelligent characters unlike the usual movie perception of Germans as dimwitted Nazi barbarians. The new project met with disapproval not only from the War Office – who withdrew all support for the picture – but Prime Minister Winston Churchill himself, who made strenuous efforts to prevent the film from being completed and later obstructed its release outside Britain.

Inspired by a scene deleted from *One of Our Aircraft is Missing*, *The Life and Death of Colonel Blimp* was Powell and Pressburger's most ambitious work thus far. Pressburger explained that the earlier film was to have contained an exchange between George Corbett (Godfrey Tearle) – 'resented by the younger members of the crew. They thought he was too old for the job, but of course he had some wisdom which they could use' – and youngest crew member Haggard (Hugh Burden) in which the older man reflects that although of different generations they are both very much alike. 'You come from the same kind of background – somehow you feel that in the future you might one of these days be like me'. This was the starting point of the new story which along the way took on the idea of utilizing David Low's 'Colonel Blimp' image from the *Evening Standard* cartoon. 'Take Blimp, bring him together with the younger generation', said Emeric, 'so that the younger man forgets that Blimps are not born, Blimps have been made'. David Low, 'a very gentle fellow although his cartoons used to be very vicious', agreed entirely to this use of his creation.

With Rank this time agreeing to back the film – atoning for the *Aircraft* débâcle the Ministry of Information approved the script, and Laurence Olivier agreed to play the leading role of Clive Wynne Candy. As the use of army equipment was required, formal approval was needed from the Ministry of War, and from here on, things ran less smoothly. After reading preliminary outlines of the story, the War Office refused to co-operate and Prime Minister Winston Churchill was alerted.

The Life and Death of Colonel Blimp is essentially a love story which along the way suggests that British Army tactics were out of touch with reality, with Generals playing a gentleman's war to set rules. As if that were not enough for the Ministry, there was also a deep friendship between a British and a German soldier stretching over a period of 40 years. The Archers, and Pressburger in particular, were labelled in some quarters as pro-German. Emeric told Kevin Gough-Yates in November 1970:

I wanted to express this feeling of mine that although my mother had died in the concentration camp and I was preconditioned about the whole thing… that there are also good Germans though the great majority of them proved to be pretty awful. But there were still Germans… who didn't have to go away from Germany but chose to go.

The Ministry objected to the film's view of both the British Army and its outdated, 'Blimpish' officers and the German characters whose 'thug element is ignored'. The withdrawal of military equipment was an inconvenience quickly solved – 'we stole it', said Powell – but Olivier's release from the Fleet Air Arm was now also refused, obviously with the intention of scuppering the production altogether. Powell immediately cast Roger Livesey, then working in an aircraft factory from where he would not need Ministry approval.

The three women in Candy's life – his 'ideal' – would be played by one actress. First choice Wendy Hiller became pregnant before shooting began and Powell made the bold but inspired choice of casting 20-year-old Deborah Kerr who, cut from *Contraband* two years earlier, had since been seen in *Major Barbara* and *Love on the Dole*.

Anton Walbrook eagerly agreed to star in the film, having himself fled from Nazi rule in Europe before finally settling in England in 1937. 'He knew what we were driving at', said Powell. 'Also he'd actually been an enemy alien in England. He wanted to play in something to show that he was on the right side, which he was'. The eloquent and moving scene in which Walbrook's character is questioned by immigration officers during the Second World War was actually drawn from Emeric Pressburger's experiences as an 'enemy alien' in wartime Britain, but also accurately reflected the actor's own views. Five years later, signed to a film called *Dice of Fate*, he was introduced to co-star Lida Baarova – said to be Goebbels' favourite actress – and reportedly 'stood speechless for a moment and then said, "I do not know this lady"'. before walking out of the restaurant and the movie. The report added 'Mr Walbrook... considered it an "offence" to his "human and artistic dignity" to have been suggested as a costar of Miss Baarova'.

Blimp faced further problems when on 8 September 1942 a memo from Secretary of State for War Sir James Grigg to Winston Churchill mentioned 'the *Blimp* film... which I think it of the utmost importance to get stopped'. The Ministry approached J. Arthur Rank to 'bring home... the fact that it is viewed with disfavour by the War Office and that no Army facilities will be available'. Churchill responded by asking Minister of Information Brendan Bracken, 'Pray propose to me the measures necessary to stop this foolish production before it gets any further. Who are the people behind it?'

Bracken suggested that a direct appeal from the Prime Minister to the filmmakers would be the best approach, only for Churchill to offer him 'any special authority you may require' to halt the film. The Cabinet agreed to postpone a decision until the film had been seen by the War Office, by which time (May 1943) the MoI felt it 'unlikely to attract much attention or to have any undesirable consequences on the discipline of the Army'. Churchill, however, considered the film 'disgraceful' following its Charity Premiere on 10 June. Ordering that overseas distribution be blocked, he managed to prevent the picture's US release despite appeals from Rank who, by mid July, wrote in an official capacity to the MoI requesting the film be accorded the usual means of export. Bracken supported the request, reassuring Churchill that 'the film is so boring I cannot believe it will do any harm abroad to anyone except the company which made it'.

Still Churchill remained immovable while the weary Bracken bemoaned 'If we had left this wretched film alone it would probably have proved an unprofitable undertaking, but by the time the Government has finished with it there is no knowing what profits it will have earned'. By mid-August Rank pressed further, announcing that the film had 'broken all previous box-office records for the Odeon circuit of cinemas'. The ministry appealed to the Prime

● The start of a beautiful friendship – Anton Walbrook (left) and Roger Livesey as Theo Kretschmar-Schuldorff and Clive Wynne Candy in *The Life and Death of Colonel Blimp*. Churchill was unamused.

Minister that it was 'becoming practically impossible to maintain our illegal ban', and overseas release was finally approved on 25 August 1943, although it was May 1945 before the film was seen in the US in a print cut by about 20 minutes.

Blimp was to suffer probably more than any other Archers film from differing release prints. The original 163 minutes had already been cut by Powell due to a shortage in Technicolor stock. Several versions eventually circulated; a 120-minute print dispensed entirely with the opening sequence and ran the story from 1902 onwards. In the mid-1970s, the BBC and National Film Archive jointly produced a new 158-minute print, seen in London in 1978, which was later extended with help from the Rank Organisation and the Sainsbury Charitable Trust to the complete original length. This version was finally premiered in America on 8 July 1988, opening a two-week season of Powell-Pressburger movies in New York, where it was puzzlingly hailed by critics as 'England's answer to *Citizen Kane*'.

Less controversially, as members of Independent Producers – who also included Frank Launder and Sidney Gilliatt, Cineguild (David Lean and Ronald Neame) and Ian Dalrymple – The Archers' next venture was to be a 40-minute recruiting film, *The Volunteer*, suggested by Ralph Richardson who, as a member of the Fleet Air Arm, explained that the service evidently felt neglected by comparison with the Army, Navy and Air Force. *The Volunteer* was made quickly but not without some difficulty: much of the filming took place on board aircraft carrier *Indomitable* which was at sea and likely to engage in action at any time. Other locations were the New Theatre and Denham Studios – not the normal stages but the offices and commissary, where Laurence Olivier made a brief appearance pretending to be a fish. Michael Powell was seen in the role of a photographer outside Buckingham Palace following the presentation of 'Fred's' medal. A successful recruiting piece, of which Powell later remarked 'We were told it did a good job. Nobody got a CBE or anything'. Most satisfying for Emeric Pressburger was the experience of 'shooting *The Volunteer* in the streets of London when I bought an *Evening Standard* and saw that I had won the Oscar [for *49th Parallel*]. It was the first I had heard about it at all!'

A Canterbury Tale followed in 1944, and became the duo's first critical and box-office failure. Perhaps Powell's most personal and misunderstood film, set in and around his beloved Canterbury where Pressburger, as a Hungarian with a stateless passport, was denied permission to work, its plot told of a mysterious figure who pours glue on to girls' hair to prevent them going out with visiting American soldiers. At the heart of the film lies a deep love of England, its heritage and its future, epitomized by the efforts of the 'glueman' to educate people to the natural beauty around them. The mystical quality and poetic vision of the film is only now being fully recognized, but in 1944 there were few willing to accept a fanatical poet figure expounding his philosophy on life, even if it dealt with the very qualities which the country was then fighting for. Fifty years on, another strand of the story becomes clear: with society at last waking up to the care and preservation of the endangered countryside, *A Canterbury Tale* has strong claims to be the first environmentally aware film.

On a spiritual level too the film has strong qualities, brought to light during Colpepper's lantern-slide lecture and again in the fields above Chillingbourne. Alison fancies that she hears the sounds from long-gone pilgrims mounting the Old Road to Canterbury, although Colpepper insists that 'those sounds come from inside not outside'.

Casting included Esmond Knight in three roles: first as Narrator, speaking from Chaucer's *Canterbury Tales*, and later in two small comic roles – one a British soldier comparing notes with Bob Johnson, and the other in a hilarious scene as a Village Idiot. Of the leading players, apart from Eric Portman in a role refused by Roger Livesey who evidently considered the part distasteful, the remaining three performers were all making their screen debuts: Sheila Sim inherited the role of Alison the Land Girl intended for Deborah Kerr, now under contract to MGM. Dennis Price was to become a popular ingredient in many British productions of the next 30 years, while for the story's American soldier, Powell discovered non-professional actor John Sweet, a US Army Sergeant, appearing in a touring production of *Our Town*. The surprise hit of the picture, John Sweet gained excellent reviews; this was to be his only screen appearance and he returned to teaching in America after the war.

Beautifully photographed and lit by Erwin Hillier, *A Canterbury Tale* contains some of the most memorable images in all Powell and Pressburger's productions, in particular the lecture sequence lit almost entirely by means of a lantern slide projector. Eric Portman carries most of the scene single-handed, much of it in silhouette against the circle of light behind him, an eerie man-in-the-moon figure. The outdoor sequences, too, are attractively filmed, as noted by several reviewers.

Allan Gray's evocative music score perfectly captures the spiritual, mystical quality of the story, switching from Colpepper's half-imagined pilgrims to the modern day. Art Director Alfred Junge produced remarkable sets, not least the interior of Canterbury Cathedral itself. The real cathedral had removed all of its stained glass windows for the duration of the war, so a monumental set was built at Denham, as were scale models of the bell tower for the opening and closing sequences shot against the swinging bells – pulled, incidentally, by the actual cathedral bell-ringers.

Critics, however, complained of a confusing storyline and poor taste concerning the character of the 'glueman', particularly as he remains apparently unpunished at the film's close. There were even claims of immorality over Alison's admission to Colpepper that she had spent a caravanning holiday with her fiancé.

Not released in the United States until January 1949, the picture had been cut from 124 minutes to 95 yet included additional scenes not seen in the

English release. The American version lost the evocative opening shots of pilgrims heading for Canterbury and the imaginative and spectacular transformation of a swooping falcon into an aircraft on a training exercise 600 years later (a device adapted by Stanley Kubrick for *2001: A Space Odyssey* in 1968). Instead the film opened on the top of a skyscraper where a former GI (John Sweet) tells the story in flashback to his bride (Kim Hunter). Much of the poetic beauty of the film was lost with the removal of scenes of the countryside and the way of life in rural England. For some years this was the only available version until the 1977 restoration financed by the National Film Archive.

Powell's explanation for the film's failure modified over the years. In 1971 he claimed that 'it contained some of my favourite sequences [but] it was one of Emeric's most complicated ideas and I really let him down for not insisting that it was simplified... It was much too complex a story'. Seven years later, he told *Sight and Sound*:

The idea was to examine the values for which we were fighting... partly through the eyes of a young American who was training in England. That's where we guessed wrong, because by the time the film came out all the Americans were off fighting in North Africa... So it was a failure and practically hasn't been seen until recently. Now it looks a wonderful film, I think. I was really thrilled with it. It's got all the things I knew so well... there's a lot of a little boy growing up in the film.

By 1983, Powell still maintained that 'we had misjudged this one', although favourable reviews of the restored print had given him second thoughts: 'We had been on the defensive about *A Canterbury Tale* for so long that even we were surprised.'

The care evident in this production should have guaranteed Powell and Pressburger another huge success, but even 50 years later it remains a much misunderstood picture, although Steven Spielberg is among those who rightly considers it a 'wonderful film'; one of the most remarkable and unique in British cinema.

The Sidneyan Society – first professed aim: to 'help enlighten public opinion on the effect of film, radio and television on the minds of nations' – now launched a remarkable, sustained attack on the works of Powell and Pressburger in their pamphlet *The Shame and Disgrace of Colonel Blimp – The True Story of the Film*. Pointedly naming the duo 'Pressburger-Powell' – thus implying an overriding 'Germanic' influence – they claimed that 'the process... started with the German hero Captain in *The Spy in Black*', before dissecting each subsequent film for supposed 'anti-Britishness'.

They noted 'contempt for the British' in *The Spy in Black* through Conrad Veidt's portrayal as the German spy 'bashing our people about all over the

● Denied permission to enter Canterbury as an 'enemy alien' during the war, Emeric Pressburger instead had Canterbury come to him. He and Powell are pictured on the staircase of the massive cathedral set on Stage Four at Denham.

place' and being allowed 'a hero's death', before moving on to *49th Parallel* and accusations of 'muddle-hearted European custom' in 'placing the Nazis in the forefront'. Even film titles were targets for their outrage. 'Notice the emphasis', they urged. 'One of *ours* is missing, not one of *theirs*'. In fact, *One of Our Aircraft is Missing* was dedicated to the bravery of the Dutch resistance movement whose work at great personal risk had liberated many British from the occupied territories. The *New Statesman* reviewer recognized this, adding 'I find no subject more moving than the never-ceasing war waged by the occupied countries against their oppressors. Here we have it presented with deep feeling and consummate skill'. Evidently this was not good enough for the Sidneyans, who next turned to *A Canterbury Tale* as the latest 'slap in the face' to the British. 'Nothing less than Canterbury… the very heart of all that has made the English speaking world stand firm in upholding the right against the forces of evil', they claimed, 'nothing but the finest, the highest, the noblest has to be made the scene of a most puerile, piffling and pathological story of a vicious split-minded personality'.

Michael Powell had already responded to the society's criticisms of *49th Parallel* in the *Dumfries Standard*, stating 'our intention was that it should be seen and heard by the widest possible audience and provoke sincere discussion and thought'. Unconvinced, the Sidneyans merely misquoted the proverb in reply, 'The road to hell is paved with such sincerity'.

A Canterbury Tale was followed by, on the face of it, a more modest film, *I Know Where I'm Going!* though this charming and romantic story has rightly attracted many followers over the years. It again returned to one of Powell's favoured settings – remote islands, raging seas and the mystical qualities of local legends.

If the 'crusade against materialism' of *A Canterbury Tale* had failed, Powell suggested that they 'have another go at it', and Pressburger took a remarkable five days to produce the complete original story of *I Know Where I'm Going!*: a love story complete with elements – apart from the elements themselves – of 'ancient' seafaring legends and local eccentricities. Powell, meanwhile, scouted locations in the Hebrides, finally settling on Jura.

Wendy Hiller – having been replaced by Deborah Kerr in *The Life and Death of Colonel Blimp* – now gave her best-ever screen performance in a role ironically intended for the now-unavailable Kerr, although she does not retain fond memories of the filming. 'Michael Powell was a brilliant film-maker', she says, 'but I found him an unsympathetic character. He was entirely ignorant about acting, and not very interested in the needs and conditions that an actor works under'.

James Mason promised to be a darkly romantic Torquil but withdrew either in a dispute over billing or, most probably, owing to likely conditions when filming in a remote Scottish outpost in October during wartime. Powell claimed the star 'didn't propose to play Boy Scouts for anybody', while Mason

● Wendy Hiller examines the map of Kiloran, the honeymoon island she will never reach in *I Know Where I'm Going!*, with 'that darling creature', Roger Livesey.

wrote that 'Powell let it be known that we would live in camping conditions – hutments, cottages or tents and that although we would never be shooting beyond a radius of thirty miles from Tobermory... we could not use its hotel accommodation because no transportation would be available'. Mason argued that he and wife Pamela could travel back with the day's film – 'it was our war aim to stay together and, if necessary, be demolished by the one bomb' – but 'Powell would not budge. I think that he was not very keen on overloading his unit with wives or husbands who were there strictly as passengers'. Wendy Hiller recollects the actual conditions as 'very comfortable but bare. We had a very old empty house which had been requisitioned by the Army and then given back to us. It was a bit like being in the Army really'.

Roger Livesey again stepped in despite being contracted to a West End play; his close-ups were shot in the studio, with a stand-in doubling for him in the Highlands. The device worked remarkably well – only the eagle-eyed would spot the doppelganger on Mull – so James Mason could have filled the same duties without ever having to leave London. Wendy Hiller, however, was delighted to be working with Livesey, having 'been in love with him long before I met him'. She recalls him as 'a darling creature and a charming man [who] made everything very smooth. I think Michael Powell liked working with him because he made what the director should have been making – the right atmosphere on the set'. The two worked well together as the ill-matched pair: remarking on how poor the local people are, Joan is told 'They're not poor. They just don't have any money'. Increasingly torn by her feelings for Torquil, the planned marriage to Bellinger is finally shattered with the symbolic loss of her wedding dress overboard during the failed voyage towards Kiloran.

Briefly seen in a minor role was 12-year-old Petula Clark. 'Michael Powell scared the wits out of me', she says, although 'he was kinder to me than with some of the actors. I knew, however, that I was working on a good film, with a great director and I felt glad that I'd had the experience. Seeing the movie again I realise just how delicate a touch he had. Romantic too – in the real sense of the word'. Wendy Hiller agrees. 'It's romantic in an unsentimental way', she says, adding 'Although I was in it, I should say [the film] was one of [Powell's] best. It has a charm which is lacking in many of his other technically perfect films'.

The remaining cast included Pamela Brown in her second film for Powell and – inevitably, in the director's third movie with a Scottish setting – John Laurie and Finlay Currie. Also seen as falconer Colonel Barnstaple was Esmond Knight's animal trainer uncle Captain C.W.R. Knight, although Esmond argued that he could have played his own uncle far more convincingly!

I Know Where I'm Going! was better received than *A Canterbury Tale*, although some reviewers were surprised at the apparent slightness of the storyline – having complained of the previous film's complexity. It was not seen in America until August 1947, almost two years after its UK release. A 1986 restoration by the National Film Archive saw its reissue and it was made available on home video in 1991.

As the war at last drew to a close, Powell and Pressburger were asked by Jack Beddington, head of the Ministry of Information Films Division, to consider a story promoting good relations between Britain and America. The result was *A Matter of Life and Death*: a fantastic story of the workings of the human mind tied together by an Anglo-American love story. With many of their usual collaborators including production designer Alfred Junge, costume designer Hein Heckroth and, particularly, cameraman Jack Cardiff, the resulting film has come to be perhaps the most popular of the Archers' works.

Powell had already chosen David Niven as the hero, although Stewart Granger – then shooting Gabriel Pascal's *Caesar and Cleopatra* at Pinewood – was briefly considered. Marius Goring also had designs on the part but was persuaded to accept the role of the Conductor which in turn had been sought by Peter Ustinov.

David Niven had returned to England at the outbreak of war, but was still under contract to Sam Goldwyn who loaned him out at large fees to Carol Reed for *The Way Ahead*, and now to The Archers for probably his finest role. Betty Field, seen in *Of Mice and Men* and *The Southerner*, was briefly considered

● David Niven's finest screen role – Peter D. Carter, poet and pilot in *A Matter of Life and Death*.

for the leading female role until, at Alfred Hitchcock's suggestion, Powell and Pressburger 'discovered' Kim Hunter. Roger Livesey further demonstrated his versatility in his third Archers film, being again radically different in appearance and wholly convincing in his part, while Raymond Massey replied to Powell's cabled offer of a role with a brief but typically warm 'For The Archers, anytime, this world or the next'.

Jack Cardiff was to be Lighting Cameraman and Director of Photography, with Geoffrey Unsworth as Camera Operator. Cardiff had made a few short features but at this time had little experience of major productions. 'I was working on the second unit of *The Life and Death of Colonel Blimp*', he later wrote. 'I realised Michael Powell had come on the small stage and was studying what I'd done. He turned to me and said "Would you like to photograph my next picture?" "Oh, yes, Mr Powell", I said. "Right", said Micky, "it will be next year", and he'd gone'. Three years later, working on the second unit of *Caesar and Cleopatra*, Cardiff 'received a telegram: "Where the hell are you? We start in three weeks". I got permission to leave immediately, and that was my break'.

Christopher Challis began his long association with the Archers on this picture. A second unit cameraman on *The Thief of Bagdad*, he had just been demobilized by the RAF and was invited by Cardiff to head a unit on *A Matter of Life and Death*. 'I completed that, and at about that time, Geoffrey Unsworth had an offer to light a film', he says. 'Michael – in his typically generous way – said they mustn't stand in his way, and I took over and finished the picture, and that's how I got started with them'.

Filming the story – set in two worlds – it was decided that one should be in colour and the other black and white, and with typical Archers perversity, 'Heaven' would be monochrome. There was some logic to the choice, Emeric irrefutably stating that while we know this world is in colour, what of the Other? Seamless transitions from colour to black and white were achieved by shooting the entire film on Technicolor stock, with relevant sequences printed without colour dyes, achieving perfect results without cuts and other trick effects.

Such a tale demanded to be filmed on a grand scale, and every effort was made to create sets equal to the magnitude of the subject. Alfred Junge and Hein Heckroth designed the great moving stairway between the two worlds, a gigantic escalator of 106 steps, 20 feet wide which took almost three months to build, while the High Court scene in the Other World was filmed on a huge set (350 ft by 40 ft), filled – at Powell's suggestion – with extras drawn from RAF Clubs, Red Cross Nurses and American WAACs.

Robert Arden – later star of Orson Welles' *Confidential Report (Mr Arkadin)* – visited his friend Kim Hunter one day and found Michael Powell 'charming, witty, friendly and quite took over the conversation – that is, until David Niven joined us. Niven, of course, was the kind of man who dominated any company'. By the time lunch was over, 'Powell asked me if I would like to be in the picture. Within an hour I was in wardrobe being measured for a uniform'. Three days later, the scene – the comic *A Midsummer Night's Dream* rehearsal at the US air base – was filmed. 'We were given full rein to ad lib the whole bit. Robert Atkins (the Shakespearean producer) played the Vicar. It was fun then, and remembering it is fun now'. Of the director, Arden recalls 'On set Powell was inclined to be autocratic, but I must say that he was, at least as far as those few days were concerned, polite, encouraging and friendly'.

Emeric Pressburger's script is one of his best: a blazingly literate and intelligent screenplay in which art, as so often, plays an important role – Peter Carter is not only an RAF pilot, but a rising poet. When Dr Reeves pleads for the English character as exemplified by John Donne, Coleridge, Wordsworth, Keats and Shelley, he asserts that Carter could be such a poet – given the opportunity. 'The boy has a fine mind', Reeves tells the surgeon. 'That's the trouble, it's too good a mind. A weak mind isn't strong enough to hurt itself. Stupidity has saved many a man from going mad'.

In 1946 the British Film Industry reached agreement with Buckingham Palace on the idea of a Royal Film Performance each year, intended to further boost the home industry. *A Matter of Life and Death* became the first ever Royal Film, screened at the Empire, Leicester Square on 1 November. Powell recalled the occasion as 'so exciting that the film passed practically unnoticed', but several critics the following day expressed doubts over the evening's success.

The *Daily Graphic* called it an 'unhappy choice' and predicted 'widespread indignation at… a picture which might have been made specially to appeal to Isolationist and anti-British sentiment in the United States', referring to a scene in which Raymond Massey's anti-British counsel points to 'faults' in the nation's character – a scene played largely for comedy, although the *Graphic* felt that 'there are in the United States today certain elements which will be only too eager to exploit it'.

The *Tribune* called the film 'spectacularly unsatisfying' owing to 'the complete absence of… the dramatic link with real-life people and their problems', ignoring that Powell and Pressburger's films were works of fantasy: cinematic poems of love, humour, eccentricity and often quite astonishing beauty. *A Canterbury Tale* had been a mystic celebration of all things British which the critics had completely failed to understand. (In fairness, they were not alone in being perplexed. Powell's first choice actor for the role of Culpepper, Roger Livesey, had claimed that he could not make any sense of it!) Now with *A Matter of Life and Death*, the press complained of the old 'faults': unreality at a time when gritty realism was what British cinema did best.

Nevertheless, Michael Powell claimed the film as his own favourite work, and the public voted the film a great success; the *Daily Mail* National Film Awards for the year placed *A Matter of Life and Death* in fifth place, behind *The Courtneys of Curzon Street*, *Great Expectations*, *Odd Man Out* and *Jassy*. Raymond Massey's son Daniel – himself later to work with Powell – hails *AMOLAD* (as it was referred to by the Archers crew) as 'one of the most brilliant and astonishing films ever made about the workings of the human mind and spirit', while Michael Winner adds 'I was brought up on his films and saw *A Matter of Life and Death* some fifty times. It still stands as one of the most extraordinary pictures ever made'.

Paradoxically it was the American press which most appreciated the quality of the film, with *Variety* claiming 'There is little, if anything in the Hollywood product of this year to surpass it'. However, Universal decreed that no film hoping for success could afford to have 'death' in the title. Despite Powell and Pressburger's objections, the March 1947 US release title became *Stairway to Heaven*.

Many British critics now seemed to take a stand against The Archers as a matter of course – a typical national trait, as William Morris had noted in 1856: 'It was always so,' he wrote. 'It is so with Ruskin; they petted him at first... but as his circle grew, embracing more and more the truth, they more and more fell off from him, his firm faith in right they call arrogance and conceit now'. In a lesser vein, Powell's career would follow the same pattern: acclaim for more conventional films was now replaced by sniping remarks as pictures like *Colonel Blimp* attempted to pinpoint faults in army methods and *A Canterbury Tale* sought to promote the quality of life in England, only to be labelled tasteless and vulgar. As autonomous producers, The Archers were also considered little more than upstart mavericks, beyond the control of any studio.

This fierce independence had enabled Powell and Pressburger to produce precisely the films they had wanted to make throughout the 1940s, supported either by Korda, Lady Yule or J. Arthur Rank. Their only abandoned projects of this period appear to have been *Fathers and Sons* – the story of the Cunard shipping line – and a 1946 romance about Bonnie Prince Charlie with David Niven and Pamela Brown. Although a colour test was shot for *The White Cockade*, the film was never made, although Niven did finally appear in the title role of Anthony Kimmins' *Bonnie Prince Charlie* two years later.

In 1946 The Archers, together with the other partners in Independent Producers, left Denham Studios and moved to Pinewood, where, for the first time in eight years, Powell and Pressburger prepared to adapt a story by another writer for the screen. Rumer Godden's *Black Narcissus* had been brought to their attention in 1942 by actress Mary Morris, but such an exotic film demanded colour and there was none to be had until the end of the war.

Powell now made the immediate – and, some felt, slightly potty – decision to create an entire Himalayan location within the studio through ingenious art direction and special effects under the control once again of the masterly Alfred Junge, despite the obvious opportunities for spectacular landscape shots in the Himalayas. In the event, Jenny Laird feels that, 'There was such a feeling of India on the marvellous sets – interior and exterior – I doubt that anything was lost by shooting at Pinewood. In fact, a lot of trouble was probably avoided – stomach bugs, diet, transport, the difficulty with processing rushes and so on'.

Apart from Pinewood, the only exterior work was at a house and gardens at Leonardslee in Horsham, Sussex, but so successful was the overall effect that there were many who collared Powell years later insisting that they had visited the exact Himalayan village where *Black Narcissus* had been shot.

Powell's decision, however, did not meet with universal approval. 'I had laid down in the

● Jenny Laird in *Black Narcissus* as the beloved Sister Honey.

contract that a unit should go to India and that I should be consulted', recalls Rumer Godden. 'They did not use one foot of Indian film, and never did anything I said!' Nevertheless, she admits, 'One could not help liking Michael Powell. He had great charm and was undoubtedly an outstanding director, but *Black Narcissus* was an unhappy experience for me'. The main difficulty was that Powell 'saw the book as a fairy tale, while for me it was utterly true... There is not an atom of truth in the film', although she does concede 'I have never had a more marvellous cast'.

To play Sister Clodagh, it was briefly suggested that Greta Garbo be approached although Garbo had been away from the cinema for six years and would never return. Instead, arrangements were made to release Deborah Kerr from her new MGM contract for 12 weeks before she left for Hollywood. Others in the cast included Kathleen Byron, startling as the neurotic sister Ruth and still recognized in the street 40 years later as 'that mad nun', Esmond Knight, Sabu and Jean Simmons, only 17 years old but a veteran of *The Way To The Stars, Caesar and Cleopatra* and *Great Expectations*. While making *Black Narcissus*, she was simultaneously filming *Hamlet* with Laurence Olivier. For Rumer Godden, she 'perfectly fulfilled my description of Kanchi, the young Nepalese girl – 'like a basket of fruit piled high, luscious and ready to eat'.

Jenny Laird 'loved working with [Powell]. I liked the amused look in his eyes and his leaping imagination – Sparks flew off him!'. She admits, however, that 'I shouldn't like to have quarrelled with him. He could be impatient, even ruthless, if somebody didn't seem to be concentrating'. As for Powell's direction:

● One of cinema's most touching and romantic farewells – David Farrar bids goodbye to
Deborah Kerr's Sister Clodagh at the close of *Black Narcissus*.

I don't remember any long discussions about character or motivation. He simply expect-
ed people to know their jobs and get on with them. He would sometimes shoot questions
at us, out of the blue: 'Miss Laird' – he always used the courtesy title 'Miss' to his actress-
es – 'Where do you think Sister Honey comes from?' I replied at random, 'Muswell Hill'.
I doubt if he had any notion where she came from, but this made him laugh. He simply
wanted to know if I knew – which I didn't, till then!

David Farrar 'had met [Michael Powell]... and was mightily impressed by his
revolutionary ideas; for a long time I felt that the talkie film had not found its
right form of expression, and [he] was nearer to knowing what that form
should be than anyone else I had met'. Farrar had been on screen since the
mid-1930s, often as a minor villain, and had recently made two films for
Ealing Studios: *Went the Day Well?* and *For Those in Peril*. Powell spotted him in
one of Vernon Sewell's films at Teddington and was so impressed that Farrar
became the first (and only) actor ever to be placed under contract by The
Archers, for three films. After reading 'an almost perfect screenplay', the actor
could hardly believe his luck at being offered the leading role in *Black Narcissus*.
'Such an opportunity was surely too good to be true', he said, with 'every day
of shooting... an exciting adventure, due to the creative ideas which were
evolved (mainly by Micky)... the constant expectation of what new ideas [he]
would produce next, kept the pulse racing'. The morally ambiguous Dean has
an unsettling effect on the nuns: bare-chested or the worse for drink in the

presence of the unworldly sisters; mischievously asking Clodagh as she eyes the erotically-posed Kanchi, 'You're sure there isn't something you're dying to ask me?' Farrar later wrote, 'I do not think I have ever been sorrier to part with a character than I was to shed the mantle of Mr Dean'.

Though emotionally charged, the screenplay is not without its lighter moments, supplied mainly by Esmond Knight's Old General ('They will eat sausages!') and the Young General (Sabu) who, on requesting admittance to the school, announces his proposed timetable of studies to include 'Mathematics by the Mathematical Sister, French or Russian by the French or Russian sisters (if any) and Physics by the *Physical* Sister!'

Described by the *Sunday Express* as 'certainly one of the most beautiful films ever made', *Black Narcissus* was highly praised for its stunning photography which occasioned a minor dispute with the Technicolor company whose control over the process at that time was total. '[Powell] encouraged me to go ahead with any idea, however wild', recalled Jack Cardiff. 'Nothing was too risky for him, and I always knew if I tried something dodgy he'd back me up to the hilt'. On *Black Narcissus* the cameraman 'used a fog filter on a very important sequence. At that time, fog filters were taboo with Technicolor and they telephoned Michael and said the sequence was ruined. When we saw the rushes, Micky said it was wonderful: "Just what I wanted". And he told Technicolor not to be so ridiculous'. Other camera tricks included the use of glass shots and miniatures, and an early morning effect of the Himalayas as a background was achieved by using a negative image of the mountain and sky – such an effective visual that it escaped critical attention.

Also notable was Brian Easdale's music score. Powell had long been intrigued by the potential influence of a music score on a scene, and planned to experiment with what he called a 'composed film': writing the music first and then shooting the film to fit. Small sections of Orson Welles' *Citizen Kane* had been handled this way, but Powell aimed to demonstrate just how effective a score could be when allowed to 'control' the action.

The climactic sequence from Ruth's rejection by Dean to her return to the convent and attempt to kill Clodagh is entirely without dialogue, the music carrying the action as Ruth stalks Clodagh in the chapel and on to the balcony. Powell and Easdale rehearsed the actors with stopwatches, trimming or elongating movements so that the edited scene would exactly fit the written score. 'It worked!' wrote Powell. 'I have never enjoyed myself so much in my life… I swore that this was the only way to make films'. Although he used the technique on later films, it is on *Black Narcissus* that Powell achieved his greatest success with this method of working.

Described by Powell simply as 'well made', *Black Narcissus* became one of the most honoured of The Archers' films. Powell well knew just how good a movie it was – he later told Jenny Laird 'You were all inspired in *Black Narcissus*'. Academy Awards went to Jack Cardiff (Best Colour Cinematography) and Alfred Junge (Best Colour Art Direction and Set

Decoration), although neither the film, its director nor any of the leading players received a nomination.

The Catholic National Legion of Decency raised objection to the film: 'The character of this film and the attitudes displayed therein create an impression that constitutes an affront to religion and religious life. It ignores the spiritual motivation which is the foundation and safeguard of religious life, and it offensively tends to characterise such life as an escape for the abnormal, the neurotic and the frustrated'. J. Arthur Rank countered that the picture had been passed by the industry's own strict Production Code Administration as well as the New York State Education Department. Nevertheless, for some American release prints all the flashbacks of Sister Clodagh's love affair in Ireland before taking her vows were removed.

Other Rumer Godden works later filmed include Jean Renoir's *The River* (1951) and *The Greengage Summer,* filmed by Lewis Gilbert in 1961. Following the 1986 release of a newly-restored print of *Black Narcissus* she spoke at a Grosvenor House luncheon. 'I remember the silence that fell when Rodney Ackland asked me what I felt about the film. "Only that I have taken a vow," I said, "never to allow a book of mine to be made into a film again"'.

By now The Archers had become something of a 'family' unit, with a first-class crew and leading players drawn from a 'pool' of actors with whom Powell had built a relationship. *Black Narcissus* featured Deborah Kerr, Esmond Knight, Kathleen Byron, Judith Furse and Sabu, all seen in previous Powell films, while others to be seen in several Archers productions included Raymond Massey, Roger Livesey, Pamela Brown, Googie Withers, Anton Walbrook, Eric Portman, Marius Goring and Cyril Cusack, who recalls 'I began to think that Michael had it in mind to maintain a kind of repertory company for his films, which is something I would thoroughly approve of as seeking artistic unity and continuity'. Yet at the same time, Powell was acquiring a reputation as 'something of a sadist' with his approach to some actors. 'It is possible that he excited antipathy in certain quarters', says Cusack, 'Sir Carol Reed once spoke of him to me as "a Nazi!"'.

Googie Withers had first worked with Powell in 1934. 'He was a very tough fellow', she says. 'Very abrasive. He wasn't pleasant to people on the set'. This took the form of extreme sarcasm if dissatisfied with his performers. Working with him again on *One of Our Aircraft is Missing* seven years later she found that he had not mellowed. 'A nice man, he was gentle, he was fun and he was intelligent, but somehow once on the set he became very sharp'. Others also recall this unattractive side to Powell's nature. Photographer Jack Cardiff recounted that Powell 'could be rude to lesser known actors, saying "You're not very good are you? Who's your agent?" He believed this sort of insult would prick them into a better performance, but I don't think it ever did'.

Despite this, Powell could also be a model of kindness, generosity and inspiration. 'It depended on the actor', says Bryan Forbes. 'He was always unfailingly pleasant to me, but he did have a reputation for not suffering fools or people he did not think were totally professional'. Citing Powell as 'in many ways one of my early mentors', Forbes also reveals that 'when I was horribly broke he lent me £100 and staved off starvation'. Christopher Challis also received generous help from both Powell and Pressburger during his early career but admits that the director 'could be extremely unkind, and [though] it was justified, he probably needn't have gone about it in such a way. But that was the way he worked and I don't think he could help it or that you could alter him. He was, I think, seeking criticism and creative argument. He spoiled for the "intellectual fight" and challenge, and in a way despised those who failed to stand up to him'.

Challis confirms, however, that Powell was 'incredibly loyal to people he liked'. Cyril Cusack found himself 'in four or five films of the Powell-Pressburger combine, while no other producer or director ever called on my talents for more than one – and I always thought I got on well with film directors!' Cusack also relates that 'David Niven once announced to me that he would always be ready to work with Powell because *he was exciting'*, while Jenny Laird feels that 'he may have been awkward, but what creative person isn't?' Googie Withers simply says, 'I think people knew him for his brilliance and somehow forgave him'.

Derek Twist, editor of *The Fire Raisers, The Phantom Light* and *The Edge of the World*, now 'sold' Powell and Pressburger on the novel which became the second Archers venture into production – *The End of the River*. Christopher Challis, after three years with Twist in the RAF Film Unit, was engaged as cameraman. Location work took the unit to Brazil for 12 weeks, with the picture finished off at Pinewood.

After completing *Thief of Bagdad* in 1940, Sabu had settled in America, becoming a US citizen and serving in the US Air Force. *The End of the River* was a rare British screen appearance for him. He was later to tour the UK with a circus act in 1951 before returning to Hollywood and jungle adventure films with titles like *Jaguar* and *Hello Elephant.*

In Brazil, Twist 'discovered' Bibi Férreira, a 24-year-old actress who managed her own theatre where she appeared 12 times a week while writing, producing and starring in a weekly radio show. The rest of the cast consisted largely of previously-seen Archers names including Esmond Knight, Torin Thatcher, Raymond Lovell and Charles Hawtrey.

The opening credits of *The End of the River* include a shot of a native archer firing the arrow which then thuds into the familiar target heralding another Archers production – the only time that this device was used. Aside from this, *The End of the River* is of little more than average interest. 'Even Esmond Knight as the heavy [and] Sabu as the hero, couldn't save it', said Powell. The producers' involvement with the film was minimal, as Christopher Challis explains. 'We were out of reach of producers for most of the picture and they only took an active part when it was all over, when I don't think that they were all that happy with it. It wasn't an awfully good picture'. Powell later conceded, 'We were failures as producers'.

For their first major production following *Black Narcissus*, Michael and Emeric chose an original story idea of Pressburger's loosely based on the fairy-tale by Hans Christian Anderson. *The Red Shoes* would be a film about Art with a vengeance and in particular, the ballet.

Originally written in 1937 as a starring vehicle for Merle Oberon whose dancing was to have been doubled by a professional, *The Red Shoes* had been shelved by London Films. 'It had earned me about £2,000 in salary', recalled Emeric, 'but Michael was very enthusiastic about it and we bought it back for £12,000 and Korda thought he was doing a tremendous deal... We took it apart again and reassembled it. Every character was clear in my mind because of the passage of time'.

This time only a genuine ballerina would be considered for the lead role. Powell approached Moira Shearer, a leading soloist with the Sadler's Wells Ballet under Dame Ninette de Valois in a company which included Margot Fonteyn. Miss Shearer had neither acted nor appeared in a film and, according to Powell, saw her career only in ballet, but she eventually agreed to make the picture. Today she describes Michael Powell as 'a director of great cinematic invention and originality with a gift for the unusual and fantastic', but found him to be a hard taskmaster: 'he neither understood nor respected actors and, far from creating a sympathetic atmosphere in the studio, he created the reverse. It was a damaging experience for many people'.

Coincidentally or otherwise, Moira Shearer conformed to an aspect of Powell's actresses remarked upon by more than one reviewer – Powell had an apparent obsession with redheaded women, much as Hitchcock favoured the famed 'cool blondes'. Powell denied any conscious emphasis on redheads, although he admitted, 'Red girls usually have more temperament and better complexions. Their nerves are much nearer the surface, aren't they?' Certainly the available evidence suggests a preference – Deborah Kerr, Moira Shearer, Anna Massey, Pamela Brown... 'There was a red-headed girl if ever there was one', he said. 'I find blondes on the whole insipid'.

Boris Lermontov, the ballet impresario of *The Red Shoes* – loosely based on both Sergei Diaghilev and Alexander Korda – is a megalomaniac to whom, the *Reynolds News* reviewer observed, 'lovers, husbands, and anything that stand between a ballerina and his ballet are less than vermin'. Anton Walbrook's portrayal was hailed as 'beautifully restrained... [his] eyes glitter coldly like pieces of glass, measured insults and ruthless sarcasms drop from his lips like gall'. A 'mirror-smashing' sequence with the star paid homage to an identical image in his 1935 title role in *The Student of Prague* while echoes of Powell's own early career were to be found in the casting of Jerry Verno and Eric Berry.

A complete ballet company was formed under the leadership of Robert

Helpmann – an extravagant move unheard of in movies, as was the idea of creating an entirely original ballet specifically for the film. Helpmann choreographed the piece as well as dancing a leading role, with celebrated master Léonide Massine creating his own role as the shoemaker.

The success of the 'composed' scene in *Black Narcissus* encouraged Powell to experiment further, this time with a proposed 20-minute ballet sequence rehearsed and edited to fit an already written score. Brian Easdale was again engaged, producing a hugely impressive score within a week before approaching Sir Thomas Beecham to conduct the orchestra for the *Ballet of The Red Shoes*. 'Only a true artist would have suggested handing over the baton to a greater man', wrote Powell.

Hein Heckroth became Production Designer with Arthur Lawson replacing Alfred Junge who, for once, could not produce the effects Powell required. Otherwise, much of the crew remained the same with Jack Cardiff behind the Technicolor cameras. Christopher Challis was 'determined to work on *The Red Shoes* in some capacity', even to the extent of working as Camera Operator. 'I didn't mind that in the least', he says. 'Of all the pictures we made, I enjoyed this one. It was absolutely marvellous – a tremendous experience'.

Ballet had never been a cinema box-office attraction, and *The Red Shoes* took an unswervingly artistic stance, summed up by Lermontov's conviction that 'Dancing to me is a religion'. Such sentiment was far from universal, least of all in business circles. When first shown the film by Emeric Pressburger, J. Arthur Rank and his accountant John Davis left the projection room without

● The dazzling *Red Shoes* ballet – Robert Helpmann, Moira Shearer and Léonide Massine.

a word, fearing they had lost their investment of over half a million pounds – a not insignificant sum which represented the most expensive Archers production to date. Their opinion seemed confirmed when US distributors Universal declared the picture 'would not make a penny'. Rank gave the film only a limited UK release in an attempt to recoup his money but, with such lacklustre promotion, the film failed at the box-office.

An independent US distributor now aimed their campaign at young American ballet fans and, by the end of 1950, with an unbroken 110-week run on Broadway, *The Red Shoes* had become the most successful British film of all time. Universal took over US distribution in 1951. At the Academy Awards, Oscars went to Hein Heckroth (Colour Art Direction), Arthur Lawson (Colour Set Direction) and – significantly – to Brian Easdale for his music score: *The Red Shoes* became the first British film to be so honoured, a justification of Powell's increasingly bold use of music in his movies. There were also nominations as Best Film (losing to Olivier's *Hamlet*) and Best Original Story (winner was MGM's *The Search*).

The *Daily Mail* National Film Awards, voted for by the general public, placed The Archers' film third behind *Spring in Park Lane* and *Oliver Twist*. Interestingly, Moira Shearer was named eighth most popular actress in a list including such established stars as Vivien Leigh, Valerie Hobson, Anna Neagle and Patricia Roc.

The movie's popularity and influence grew with the years. In 1951 Gene Kelly screened the Archers' film to persuade MGM to back *An American in Paris* and *The Red Shoes* is cited as inspiration by the aspiring – and perspiring – hopefuls of the long running 1980s Broadway musical *A Chorus Line*, later filmed by Richard Attenborough. A clip from *The Red Shoes Ballet* featured in the 1985 MGM compilation *That's Dancing*.

Nevertheless, British critics of 1948 complained of the film's length (136 minutes), lack of realism (the spectacular ballet) and 'poor taste'. This last criticism had dogged Powell's work since the appearance of *A Canterbury Tale*'s 'glueman'. Now, with *The Red Shoes,* objections centred on Moira Shearer's battered and bleeding body being lifted from the railway lines. In defence, Powell asked just what would people expect to see after she had been hit by a train? He recalled the Hans Christian Andersen original which inspired the story, in which the girl's feet are ultimately chopped off by a woodman's axe. By comparison, the screen ending seemed tame! Critics, however, were uneasy over whether the film was a fairy-tale or not.

Rank's lack of faith in *The Red Shoes* led Powell and Pressburger to accept Alexander Korda's offer to return to London Films and sign a five-picture deal supposedly giving them unlimited freedom of both subject and cast. For a starring vehicle for David Farrar they turned again to an outside source, settling on *The Small Back Room* by Nigel Balchin whose previously filmed work, *Mine Own Executioner* (1947), had been made for Korda by Anthony Kimmins.

● David Farrar and the much-discussed 'expressionist' sequence in Powell and Pressburger's impressive *The Small Back Room*.

A complete contrast to *The Red Shoes*, *The Small Back Room* was a realistic, at times downbeat, wartime story made in atmospheric black and white. Powell later claimed it as 'an error of judgement... nobody wanted to know about it because the war was over', although critically the film gained good notices despite the by now customary charges of vulgarity and poor taste levelled at the director. This criticism was reserved exclusively for one sequence – cut from some prints – in which Farrar hallucinates over a whisky bottle as he waits for Susan's late arrival. The bottle preys on his mind until he is wrestling with both his conscience and, literally, the bottle which has assumed fantastic proportions and finally crushes him. Several reviewers attacked the scene, the *Graphic* claiming the picture was 'marred by one piece of pretentious, impressionistic montagery... quite meaningless and totally out of place in a film otherwise refreshingly realistic'.

The scene is far superior to either the 'DTs' section in Billy Wilder's *The Lost Weekend* or the celebrated Salvador Dali-designed sequence in Alfred Hitchcock's *Spellbound*. Christopher Challis reveals 'The concept of the thing was probably Hein Heckroth. I think he suggested the idea of the clock dominating the scene and then Michael talked to me about it and together we worked out how to do it with split screens'.

Although he claimed not to like the description, preferring the term 'expressionist', Powell later agreed with Leo Maguire that 'he must be the only British Surreal film director'. Maguire's wife, Maxine Audley continues, 'Asked if he was influenced by Renoir or Buñuel, Powell was insistent that early Germans like Pabst or Murnau were much greater lights in his early life.

Powell and Pressburger were so ahead of their time – yet, the paradox is that Micky was heavily influenced by silent directors well *before* his time'.

This nightmare sequence apart, the film remained largely faithful to the novel, though including the eccentricities one might expect of an Archers film. The meeting with the military to discuss the new gun is almost entirely drowned out by the sound of road-works outside the window, and is further interrupted by the arrival of an Air Warden to complete the blackout – in daylight.

Apart from David Farrar – hugely impressive as the tormented Sammy Rice – the excellent and unusually strong supporting cast included second-billed Kathleen Byron in her fourth and final role for The Archers. Her scenes with Farrar were particularly sensuous, and several critics remarked on Miss Byron's growing reputation as an actress to watch, the *Graphic* singling her out as 'a young actress with great femininity and beautiful repose'. Also making their final appearances for Powell were Leslie Banks and Milton Rosmer, both veterans of Powell's 'quota quickies'. 'New' faces on view included Michael Gough ('a definite find', said the *News of the World*), Sidney James, Cyril Cusack in his first Archers appearance and Jack Hawkins, destined for major international stardom in a few years, suitably oily as the lecherous R.B. Waring. Future director and author Bryan Forbes made his screen debut in the film, which also briefly featured Renée Asherson in one of her all too rare screen roles. She found Powell and Pressburger 'very interesting and original film-makers; bold in their time. Michael Powell himself seemed to give a very personal quality to all his films – a sort of acid sweetness'.

The lengthy scene in which Sammy dismantles the booby-trapped bomb maintains a remarkable tension, as the *News of the World* reviewer observed. 'You are made to feel that one wrong move by David Farrar and the whole of the Empire Theatre will be dispatched to eternity. Magnificent picture making'. Christopher Challis agrees. 'I think that was one of the most marvellous sequences ever. Now that was entirely Micky – the idea of getting closer and closer as the sequence became more tense until you ended up with just fingernails and eyes and bits of the bomb screws'.

Despite his recollection of the picture as a commercial failure, Powell told French magazine *Midi Minuit Fantastique* in 1968 that *The Small Back Room* was one of his personal favourites. 'Very simply, an invalid scientist tries to discover how the bombs work', he said. 'It is also the story of a hunted man who discovers a reason for living. I think that it is my best film'. Not released in the US until February 1952, the film was cut by about ten minutes and given the rather obvious title *Hour of Glory*.

Reverting to Technicolor, The Archers turned to an ill-fated tale of Old English country mysticism, symbols and superstitions. Of all their films retitled, cut or otherwise altered for the American market, none suffered such a difficult passage as did *Gone to Earth*.

After leaving Hollywood in mid-1949, producer David O. Selznick had married his beautiful contract star Jennifer Jones in Italy, but characteristically found himself unable to remain idle. Co-producing (with Korda) *The Third Man*, he next – as a great admirer of *The Red Shoes* – duly arranged to co-present the next Archers production.

Korda already owned screen rights to the novels of Mary Webb, having planned to star Robert Donat in an ultimately unmade version of *Precious Bane*. Powell and Pressburger now proposed filming her 1917 story *Gone to Earth*, with Selznick granted North American distribution rights in return for which Jennifer Jones would star with a strong all-British supporting cast including David Farrar, Esmond Knight – giving his best ever performance as the colourful Abel Woodus – and Cyril Cusack, who found that '[Jennifer], aided and abetted by Selznick, preferred me to Paul Scofield'. James Donald was also tested for the role, but Cusack made his second picture in a row for Powell (actually his third; the already completed *The Elusive Pimpernel* was released later).

Locations were scouted on a lengthy walking tour by Michael Powell and Christopher Challis, who recalls, 'We spent a lot of time looking for locations. Of course in those days you could afford to – it was a small unit and one could do those sort of things'. Nevertheless, the use and transportation of the 'extremely heavy equipment, wind machines' and so on in such a setting often made filming difficult, although 'to [Micky] it was a challenge'.

Filming took place in the novel's setting, Much Wenlock on the Welsh border. 'The Shropshire hills threw forth an emotional flush', says Cyril Cusack.

● Jennifer Jones as Mary Webb's heroine Hazel Woodus in Powell and Pressburger's ill-fated *Gone to Earth.*

'One night I found a note slipped under my bedroom door. It said that I had taught her "a lesson" in what she called "humility", a virtue in which, whatever of its seeming presence, I am fundamentally lacking. Jennifer was very much in her part, drawn into the romantic atmosphere of the place and the novel, as was I'.

Miss Jones also took readily to working with 'Foxy', supplied and trained by Esmond Knight's cousin Jean and uncle C.W.R. Knight, even suggesting that the animal sleep in her room at night. Indeed, the film owed much to the star's courage as an actress. Having crawled over rocky landscapes and slid down mountains in *Duel in the Sun,* and been lashed by tidal waves in *Portrait of Jennie,* she was now required to climb Shropshire's hills and race across open fields and countryside, often bare-footed. Powell paid handsome tribute to her devotion: 'What a beautiful woman, great-hearted girl, inspired actress, restless soul!' A different example of this devotion is recalled by Cyril Cusack. 'Michael had Jennifer and myself kissing passionately – as it was seen in those days – over and over again, while Chris Challis, our cameraman, looked on aghast. Jennifer is still part of a romantic memory…'.

'Michael was a visual director', says Challis. 'He created the opportunities for you to be able to do it the way he wanted it in terms of waiting for the right light, going to the right locations, things like that'. Beautifully photographed, the film is filled with potent imagery, from Hazel's first entrance to her cottage framed in one of her father's half-made coffins. Clearly she is doomed from the outset. One scene in particular is worthy of mention for the simplicity with which it establishes Hazel's pure and innocent character: while singing 'Harps in Heaven' at the country fair, she absentmindedly and with childlike innocence scratches one ear as the song continues, and in that simple gesture it is clear that she has sung it a thousand times but is entirely unaware of its effect on the gathered listeners.

Twelve weeks on, filming came to an abrupt halt when the British Field Sports Society advised its members not to lend hounds to the production, claiming that Mary Webb – whose original novel had been unequivocally anti-hunt – had been inaccurate in her treatment of the 'sport'. 'In these days', they added, 'when… the public feel as they do about hunting, it's a bit hard to expect hunters to take part in a film which would unwittingly, perhaps, condemn them'. A suggestion that the story be rewritten to accommodate the BFSS was rejected by Pressburger, who remarked, 'I suppose they wanted us to let the fox chase the dogs!' The unit completed studio shots at Shepperton, returning to Shropshire three weeks later when Welsh farmer Daniel Stephens offered his pack for the film, appearing himself as Master of Fox Hounds.

Greater problems followed in March 1950 when David Selznick attempted to block the release of the movie which, he claimed, 'varied in substance' from Mary Webb's novel. In court, he cited six 'differences', typical of which was that concerning the character of Reddin: 'hard and sensual, but with a kinder side' (in the book), but 'brutal' (in the film). After reading the book and privately viewing the film, the judge – complaining that the cinema had given him a headache – ruled that as Selznick had approved the shooting script, London Films could release the picture as it stood.

Gone to Earth was released in the UK to mixed reviews – *New Statesman* dismissed it as 'the worst bit of kitsch its makers have yet produced' – and Selznick announced plans the following March to reshoot the film for American release, partly, it was claimed, to satisfy the US censors, but mainly 'to improve the picture' which would be retitled *Gipsy Blood.* Although Powell was approached to direct the new sequences, Christopher Challis says, 'Micky didn't want anything to do with it', which placed the cameraman in a quandary when invited to go to Hollywood for the reshooting. 'I talked to Michael and Emeric', he says, 'and asked, "What am I going to do? Isn't it disloyal if I go?" but they said "Well we'd much rather you did because at least there'd be somebody there to make sure it looks the same if nothing else"'.

Rouben Mamoulian directed the new footage while, as Challis recalls, 'tremendous arguments about the script caused a lot of reshooting – pretty well the whole of the end sequence and additional scenes too'. Selznick eventually discarded all but 35 minutes of *Gone to Earth,* even eliminating some characters altogether until – with yet another new title, *The Wild Heart,* and running at only 82 minutes – it was finally released in May 1952. This version differs from *Gone to Earth* by the addition of a spoken prologue (by Joseph Cotten) – a typical Selznick device – and a few non-essential plotlines, but loses much of the poetic imagery and mystical quality of Powell and Pressburger's version.

Pam Cook, in a 1986 *Monthly Film Bulletin,* asserted that 'Jennifer Jones' utterly convincing performance as the complex and divided heroine… is transformed in the reshot sequences into a virtual reprise of Pearl's steaming sensuality in *Duel in the Sun*'. Despite his undeniable reputation as a quality filmmaker, the ever-meddling Selznick was sorely lacking in terms of subtlety when preparing a screenplay, milking dialogue from literary works for the sake of 'authenticity' at the expense of the overall spirit of the piece. This clumsy, verbose approach is apparent even in his masterpiece *Gone with the Wind.* Powell's direction of *Gone to Earth,* aided by the handsome camerawork of Christopher Challis and Freddie Francis, made prologues and explanatory titles wholly unnecessary.

Despite Selznick's efforts, *The Wild Heart* failed with US audiences although, perversely, this version was released in the UK on home video in 1980, with the original unavailable until the NFA's glorious new print was seen at the 1985 London Film Festival. *Gone to Earth* was finally recognized as one of The Archers' most beautiful movies with stunning photography, superb performances and a terrific, evocative music score by Brian Easdale. In 1971 Powell considered the picture 'a disaster… except for Jennifer's performance which I thought was absolutely wonderful', feeling that they had 'never licked the script… it is doubtful if Mary Webb can be licked!' Ten years later, however, to

Films and Filming he was to call *Gone to Earth* 'a beautiful film [if] a little long-winded', claiming it as their most popular film in France, where it was released as *La Renarde* (*The Vixen*).

Gone to Earth marked the third and final Archers appearance of their contract player David Farrar. 'Now that James Mason and Stewart Granger have left the British film scene', wrote one reviewer, 'there is none to touch David Farrar in this sort of thing'. Although featuring well in other British films of the period, Farrar left for Hollywood in 1951 where he found himself cast in largely indifferent movies. In 1962 he retired from the screen and from the public eye altogether. Anglia Television tracked him to South Africa in 1986 but were unable to persuade him to appear on their programme. It is tempting – though probably wholly inaccurate – to imagine him settled in a remote village, not unlike *Black Narcissus*' Mr Dean, his own favourite screen character.

Although Korda had promised The Archers total freedom in their deal with London Films, he soon urged them to consider *The Scarlet Pimpernel,* which he had himself produced and directed (uncredited) in 1934 with a star cast including Leslie Howard, Merle Oberon and Raymond Massey. Powell and Pressburger saw no reason to remake a story which had already been definitively filmed, but Korda persisted – the film would be in Technicolor and co-produced by Samuel Goldwyn, thereby ensuring a prestige American release. Powell eventually agreed, intending to rework the story as a musical.

Still under contract to Goldwyn, David Niven was cast as The Pimpernel though keen to return to his family and home in Hollywood after completing *Bonnie Prince Charlie* in England. The star managed to delay filming by almost three months, finally breaking with Goldwyn on his return to America.

Korda, meanwhile, vetoed The Archers' musical plans, and both producers resisted any alterations to the story as suggested by the new script. Powell reflected 'if you're making a film between Goldwyn and Korda like we were you get ground to a powder', and the resulting picture became a musical screenplay devoid of the music. 'It never went right', he later admitted, although in a 1950 *Picturegoer* article he claimed, 'The old, simple romance is still one of the best stories ever told', further defending both this and *Gone to Earth*. 'Beauty, truth and the heart of England. I believe in these three things. They are in these two books, they are part of them. And they are in the two films which we made… I don't think our love will be wasted on audiences'. Despite this, *The Elusive Pimpernel* remains a disappointing and unsatisfying picture.

Samuel Goldwyn now refused to handle the movie which delayed its US release while Korda took out a lawsuit against him. The film was eventually distributed by Caroll Pictures in a black-and-white print only – a final insult, and one guaranteed to cause it to fail.

In a third picture for The Archers in quick succession, Irishman Cyril Cusack felt 'something of an outsider to the English sector', although this 'served the character' well. There was, however,

● Michael Powell offering a few singing hints to Robert Rounseville between takes of *The Tales of Hoffmann.*

one disquieting incident. I had seventeen takes because I simply could not follow the light-ing. I shall not forget the expression on Powell's face. Even the jovial Niven had begun to look tense. There was a general audible sigh of relief from all on the studio floor when at last – quite accidentally – I 'found the light'. Shortly after, Micky either – as I thought – relenting his exasperation or, more likely, all patience spent, suddenly disappeared with the instruction to me to 'direct' Niven and Margaret Leighton for the rest of the scene. It may have been meant as a punishment. Of course, I didn't dare 'direct' my fellow actors and I even forgot to say 'Cut!'

Keen to re-establish their independence within Korda's terms of contract, Powell and Pressburger met with Sir Thomas Beecham who suggested that they film Offenbach's *The Tales of Hoffmann*. The real Hoffmann, born in Koenigsberg in 1776 and raised by his uncle and grandmother, found refuge in writing bizarre tales which have been compared to those of Franz Kafka. These tales were adapted into an opera by Jacques Offenbach in 1880 as the composer's final completed work; he died just a few months before the première in February 1881. Sir Thomas had given the first UK performance of the work in 1910 and, as its leading authority, became musical director for the film, personally auditioning over 50 singers.

At Beecham's invitation, American opera star Robert Rounseville made his first trip to Europe and his film debut as Hoffmann. His only other screen role was to be in Rodgers and Hammerstein's *Carousel*, five years later. Ann Ayars also made her debut as a vocalist, despite having previously made six (non-singing) appearances under contract to MGM. All other vocals would be dubbed and mimed by dancers and actors while, in addition to most of *The Red Shoes* ballet company, the production secured the services of Sadler's Wells choreographer Frederick Ashton – his first work for the cinema.

The Tales of Hoffmann became Michael Powell's ultimate 'composed' film being, as Christopher Challis recalls, 'totally prerecorded' and then filmed and edited to the playback. Although this sounds fraught with difficulty, Challis says 'It gave us enormous freedom. We shot *Hoffmann* on what was called the silent stage at Shepperton Studios… the biggest film stage in Europe but you couldn't record sound on it'. The advantage of this was that 'We were able to talk during shooting, and we didn't have to use the huge Technicolor "blimp" [an enormous sound-proofed casing which housed the actual camera itself] – we took the camera out which made it much more mobile'. Effects work on the film was also created simply. 'Hein Heckroth, who was a stage designer with an operatic background, designed the whole thing like a stage production, and Michael decided to go back and do it all in the camera', with simple 'jump' cuts as opposed to elaborate effects.

The Tales of Hoffmann was completed in nine weeks, but what constitutes its 'final' version is open to debate. Originally listed at 127 minutes, this was cut by Powell to 115 by the removal of a spoken epilogue featuring Pamela Brown before the picture was shown at the Cannes Festival of April 1951 where it won the Special Jury Prize. Korda and – according to Powell – Pressburger suggested that the removal of the *Tale of Antonia* would secure the film the Grand Prix. Powell strongly objected, but a 96-minute version (without the third act) did initially go on release. After 'protests from hundreds of Birmingham music and ballet lovers', the complete version was seen throughout the rest of Britain. Relations with Korda, however, had already been irreversibly soured by the incident.

Inevitably the picture faced critical bias against both ballet and opera, and reviews were mixed. The *Daily Graphic* conceded that Powell and

Pressburger's 'technical brilliance… is unquestionable, and if Offenbach's *Tales of Hoffmann* had to be put on screen, I don't suppose anyone could have done it more handsomely or ingeniously… But why do it?'

Nevertheless there were signs of approval from the public, with advance bookings of £12,500 notched up in one week. In truth, there is always an inherent difficulty in filming opera, and although the ballet sequences are admirably staged and photographed, the vocal dubbing is disorientating and unsatisfactory, particularly when the same actor – Léonide Massine for instance – is dubbed by different singers in different sequences. It is hard to claim the film a complete success, although many see it as one of The Archers' finest works: *Variety* even claimed it 'a better picture than *The Red Shoes*'. Powell maintained that it was 'the film I had always dreamt about… the culmination of everything I wanted to do and show the audience'.

For the picture's American première, the New York Metropolitan Opera House was converted into a cinema for a gala screening in aid of the American Red Cross. Powell and Pressburger attended with Ludmilla Tcherina and Ann Ayars and they 'were given a rousing ovation', reported the *Daily Telegraph*, who boasted 'a British film had once more blazed a new trail in the art of screen entertainment'. This seemed confirmed at the Academy awards when Hein Heckroth was nominated for his work as both Art Director and Costume Designer. Released in 1951, the year of the Festival of Britain, the film ends on a visual joke as Beecham closes his copy of the score and rubber stamps 'Made in England' across the cover.

Frustrated by Korda's constant interference with their choice of subjects and despite their contract calling for one further film, Powell and Pressburger now bought their way out of the deal and broke with London Films. Although now free of the overpowering influence of Korda, The Archers were also without his dynamic forceful personality and found themselves unable to raise backing as easily as they had imagined.

Many likely projects were planned but discarded for a variety of reasons. *The Golden Years*, a biography of Richard Strauss, was discussed with Columbia boss Harry Cohn, who instead offered Powell the chance to film *Lawrence of Arabia*. Micky declined, only for Cohn to then reject Pressburger's completed *Golden Years* script. *Salt of the Earth*, based on the autobiography of Chaim Weizmann, a Zionist chemist who worked for the British government during the First World War, was another complete unproduced screenplay, while Powell considered *The Promotion of the Admiral*, tentatively starring Bette Davis, Gregory Peck and Roger Livesey, 'one of the two films I most regret not having made'. The Archers simply could not agree on which story should go ahead. There were 'too many films', Powell said, although paradoxically not one was made in over four years – an extraordinary delay for a partnership which had since 1939 produced at least one complete feature a year.

Instead, Michael returned briefly to the theatre where, despite depicting theatrical life so vividly on screen, his efforts as producer/director had been limited to a couple of less distinguished productions, none of which could be claimed an unqualified success.

A suggested 1943 propaganda stage version of *Henry V* starring Laurence Olivier in full battle dress had fallen through when Olivier rejected the project – 'Larry only likes ideas of his own' – and Jan de Hartog's *Skipper Next to God* had become Powell's first theatrical venture, running for a week at Windsor's Theatre Royal in 1944. Ernest Hemingway's *Fifth Column* followed, with Roger Livesey and Margaret Johnson. An over-elaborate set design – Powell later admitted he had approached the show as though it were a movie – created many difficulties and after an opening in Glasgow followed by a three-week tour, the show closed deep in debt without reaching the West End. 'I didn't get the play moving quickly enough', Michael later told one newspaper. 'But I learnt a lot'.

Six years on in December 1949, Powell now announced his intention to direct four new plays, including two by Rodney Ackland, who had been Emeric Pressburger's English dialogue coach in the early 1940s. One was to be a new version of *Dr Jekyll and Mr Hyde*, while the other – *The Pink Room* – had reportedly already 'been turned down by half the managements in London as being "too shocking"'. Neither show materialized under Powell's direction, but the autumn of 1951 saw him touring with James Forsyth's *Heloise*, starring Siobhan McKenna, Walter Machen, Mervyn Johns and Esmond Knight. For the first time Powell took a production into the West End, only to see it close after ten days. 'I'm not disheartened', he told the press. 'It's just that West End theatregoers don't seem to understand it like the people in the provinces. I might take it back to the provinces and bill it as "the play Londoners didn't understand"'.

Raymond Massey's *Hanging Judge* followed in 1952, playing first in Manchester before transferring to the New Theatre in London with Godfrey Tearle as star. Though Powell's most successful theatre work, running for two months, it proved to be his final stage venture.

In the cinema, *Twice Upon a Time*, released by London Films in 1953, saw Emeric behind the camera as director for the first – and last – time. 'I can't think why he chose that subject', says Christopher Challis, cameraman on many Archers films who also photographed this: 'It was a remake of a German film made by a friend of his a long time ago, and it really wasn't very good'. As a director, too, Pressburger was no Powell. 'He hadn't got what it takes', says Challis. 'He was too nice really, in many respects. I think he probably had the ideas but he would never ride roughshod over anyone to achieve them'.

The Archers, however, still had not made a film in over two years. *Bouquet*, suggested by Pressburger in 1953, was to be a collection of four short stories by English, Irish, Welsh and Scottish writers except that no one could agree on which four. A year later, Audrey Hepburn was set to star in *Ondine* with her husband Mel Ferrer, until Ferrer, who had directed the play on Broadway, attempted to gain control of the production. 'Emeric came up with something entirely new', said Powell. 'To do *Ondine* as a modern story, set on the French Riviera. I said "I don't know, Emeric. It's a very clever idea, but do you think Mel will like it? He hasn't got the right knees for it"'. Eventually both stars left to make *War and Peace* for King Vidor. Of his lost *Ondine* – the story of a man who falls in love with a water nymph – Powell lamented, 'I'd wanted to do a tale with a fairy princess, and we had lost our princess'.

Before decamping, Ferrer did appear in the picture The Archers finally did manage to release in 1955. Backing was finally secured for a version of Johann Strauss' operetta *Die Fledermaus*, although neither that nor its literal translation *The Bat* were considered suitable titles. *Oh, Rosalinda!!* – 'an awful title' said Powell – came from an earlier English version of the opera called *Gay Rosalinda.*

As with *The Tales of Hoffmann,* this was to be a 'composed' film with most of the actors dubbed by professional singers, although Michael Redgrave, Anthony Quayle and Anneliese Rothenberger all sang their own parts. Unlike *Hoffmann*, however, *Rosalinda* encountered 'just about every problem' according to cameraman Christopher Challis.

It was Powell's first – and last – full-length film in the CinemaScope process. Challis recalls 'It was in the early days, and the lenses then were supplementary – the CinemaScope lens was put in front of the existing camera, so you had two lenses'. This resulted in a smaller depth of field which, together with extra light needed for colour in those days, made focus a constant problem, added to which 'the colour just wasn't as good as the old three-strip. I was never happy with any of it'. Neither, it seems, were the two producers: 'I think Michael and Emeric were quite keen on it to begin with and grew to like it less and less as we started to make it'.

Even the starry cast, including Michael Redgrave, Anthony Quayle, Anton Walbrook and Dennis Price – now a major star ten years after his debut in *A Canterbury Tale* – failed to save the production. Also pencilled in at various times for roles but never actually signed to the production were David Niven, Kieron Moore, Orson Welles, Jerry Verno, Lilli Palmer, Nöel Coward, Danielle Darrieux and – improbably – Maurice Chevalier and Bing Crosby!

Somewhere towards the bottom of the final cast list was future director John Schlesinger who recalls the production as 'rather garish' and reveals something of the lot of a small-part performer in the film. 'For weeks we were drilled as the chorus, under the direction of the first assistant', he says. 'I recall a great deal of waiting about, playing a number of parts – sometimes with a toupee, sometimes not'. As for the director himself: 'I have no clear recollection of Michael Powell during those extraordinary weeks at Elstree, but I became quite friendly with Anneliese Rothenberger... to whom Powell was not very kind it seemed, as she was often reduced to tears'.

Problems were inevitable with such a project, not least by the very nature

of the material. Powell admitted that the plot was 'intentionally stupid' and, being an operetta, more akin to farce. 'You don't go out of your way to make a stupid plot in a film', he said. *Oh, Rosalinda!!* remains one of the least seen films of Powell's career, and certainly the most elusive of The Archers' productions, never theatrically released in America.

Other 'lost' projects at around this time included two further films with Cyril Cusack, who reveals that one was to have been a screen biography of Charles Dickens and the other a film of 'Paddy the Cope, the Donegal man who, along with the poet A.E. Russell, set up the Co-operative Society in his county which helped draw the people out of their poverty'. Powell had held an option on the story since the mid-1940s but, although 'Paddy Gallagher – the "Cope" – came to Pinewood and many photographs were taken of [us] striding through the studio grounds', the project finally came to nothing.

With the trials of *Oh, Rosalinda!!* behind him, Powell agreed to direct *The Sorcerer's Apprentice,* designed by Hein Heckroth, who, following his work for the Archers, was now working in German theatre. Featuring solo dancer Sonia Arova, the CinemaScope film was photographed by Christopher Challis and released by Twentieth Century-Fox in collaboration with Norddeutsher Rundfunk. A companion featurette, *The Miraculous Mandarin* failed to materialize. Emeric Pressburger had not been involved with this non-Archers production, and now suggested to Powell that they consider a conventional wartime story, *The Battle of the River Plate.*

Invited to attend the Mar Del Plata Festival in Argentina, The Archers used the trip to research the story of the Second World War incident in which the German *Graf Spee* was tricked into self destruction. The outline was optioned by Twentieth Century-Fox for an initial script advance of £5,000.

Keen to reconstruct the events at sea with full-sized ships, Powell was promised the help of the Admiralty, provided that the film crew could fit in with their schedule, and within weeks received the call that three ships were at his immediate disposal. Fox's only response was, 'Is Jack Hawkins going to play the Admiral?' Following his success in *The Cruel Sea* (Ealing, 1953), Hawkins was now considered a vital ingredient to any British film set during the war – at least as far as Hollywood was concerned.

Powell headed for South America, leaving Pressburger to placate and ultimately break with Fox, and agreement was reached with Rank, now under the leadership of John Davis, to finance and release the film. Shooting took about four months and involved location work in Malta, off the Greek Islands and Uruguay. Help was received from many sources other than the Admiralty, including the Merchant Navies of Britain, New Zealand, India, the US and Uruguay, although the Uruguayan Embassy later issued a statement denouncing the 'strange portrayal of Uruguayan life and customs that can be seen in

● Michael Powell with wife Frankie and son Columba pictured in 1957 on the set of *The Battle of the River Plate.*

the film [as] exclusively the result of the inspiration of the producers'.

The credited cast includes many familiar faces from previous Archers films – Anthony Quayle, Anthony Bushell, Michael Goodliffe, Patrick MacNee and Ian Hunter – with other leading players led by stalwart British stars John Gregson and Bernard Lee, and the rising Peter Finch as German leader Langsdorff. The cast was completed by over 100 uncredited speaking parts, all personally auditioned by Powell, including Brian Worth, Conrad Phillips, Anthony Newley, Nigel Stock, Jack Merivale and John Le Mesurier – though surprisingly not Sam Kydd, essential supporting player in dozens of British war films. John Schlesinger was to be seen in a second minor role for Powell, just prior to embarking on his own successful career behind the camera. '[Powell] was enormously encouraging and generous to me', he says, 'and I shall always remember him with the greatest affection and respect'.

Handsomely photographed in VistaVision by Christopher Challis, *The Battle of the River Plate* was chosen for the Royal Film Performance of 1956, ten years after *A Matter of Life and Death* had inaugurated the tradition. There were fewer criticisms of this choice, although some still faulted the 'sympathetic' portrayal of German characters, while others suggested that the time for making war films was over. The *Daily Herald* complained 'The heroes of this picture are a GERMAN officer and a GERMAN ship… I came away… with the impression that poor little *Graf Spee* had been hounded by three gigantic British cruisers… even seventeen years after the event, I don't think this kind of whitewash is fitting, especially at a Royal Film Performance'. Despite this, *The Battle of the River Plate* was said to be a particular favourite of Prime Minister Winston Churchill who had evidently either forgotten or forgiven the makers of 'this foolish film' (*Colonel Blimp*).

Variety reported in July 1957 with their customary subtlety that the film was now a 'B.O. Wow in Reich', quickly becoming Western Germany's top grossing picture of the year. The film – released in Europe as *The Graf Spee* – was 'the first British war pic to make a b.o. mark in Western Germany', *Variety* attributing this to 'the German naval Commander, played by Peter Finch, [who] emerged as the most sympathetic character in the film – a factor that contributed to some adverse reaction when the film was preemed (*sic*) in London'.

Peter Finch in fact proved the hit of the picture, confirming his star status following a number of increasingly impressive movies. Hans Langsdorff's widow wrote to compliment the actor on his performance, while Michael Powell felt that 'Peter had that magical thing, star quality', telling Finch's biographer Trader Faulkner, 'He gave me not only what I asked but so much more, a performance with that dimension and imagination no director can implant in a great actor. It was there in Peter, and when the camera turned on him as Langsdorff he had this subtle, sincere magic'.

Making use of the extensive research material that had accumulated during the making of the picture, Michael Powell later published the 'true' story of the incident to coincide with the film's release under the title *Graf Spee,* but of the released film, his opinion in 1971 was guarded. 'I think it was a bit stolid as a film but it seems to work marvellously', he said. Certainly it was a markedly different style of movie from the makers of *The Red Shoes* and *Black Narcissus,* being more comparable to a dramatised documentary. 'People are crazy about it, said Powell, 'but honestly, I can't understand it'.

With *Battle of the River Plate* completed, Powell – still bruised by the experience with Korda and deeply suspicious of John Davis – resisted offers to sign a long term contract with the Rank Organisation, instead agreeing to sign a one-picture deal which produced a further unlikely subject for The Archers, *Ill Met by Moonlight*, based on the book by Captain William Stanley Moss written in 1945 but not published until 1950 due to Military Intelligence restrictions.

The movie was filmed in the French Riviera where Powell had spent much of his youth, and supporting roles went to Marius Goring (in a role originally intended for Curt Jürgens) and Cyril Cusack – both on their fourth and final outing for Powell and Pressburger – with future leading players Christopher Lee and David McCallum in minor, unbilled parts. Top billing went to Rank's biggest box-office star, Dirk Bogarde. 'Powell was a marvellous friend; we knew each other well', he says today, though confirming the opinion of others before him: 'He was wonderful to me personally, though not always kind to other actors'.

Made in black and white but in the wide-screen VistaVision process used for *The River Plate,* the film bears the unique distinction for an Archers production of having been criticized by reviewers for its murky photographic quality – 'Ill lit by moonlight', wrote one. Other criticisms were raised over the extensive use of Greek and German dialogue in some scenes, devoid of English subtitles. The *Daily Mail* correspondent complained of 'too much realism', while Powell mischievously told Jympson Harman of the *Evening News*, 'This'll be all Greek to you'.

Otherwise the film was a disappointingly routine piece of wartime boys' own adventure, despite the few lighter moments: overpowering a couple of German soldiers, Dirk Bogarde asks 'What's Greek for "chloroform"?' 'Chloroform', comes the reply, while Cyril Cusack's odorous character ('I haven't washed for six months. Man of the people, I am') is established soon afterwards when a goat refuses to share a room with him! Many years later, Powell admitted he 'was surprised by how bad the film was… The script was underwritten and weak on action; the gags were unoriginal, and the surprises not surprising'.

With a hoped-for hit song based on celebrated Greek composer Mikis Theodorakis' film theme issued under the more evocative title 'Song of the Moonlight', the picture was not released in the United States until July 1958, almost 18 months after being first seen in England. By this time it had been cut from 104 minutes to 93 and acquired the less romantic and more 'gung ho' title of *Night Ambush*.

The chief historical significance, however, of *Ill Met by Moonlight* is that it marked the end of The Archers partnership after 17 years.

Frustration at having produced what he had vowed never to make – a 'programmer' – led to Powell refusing John Davis' further offer for Rank to finance either *Cassia* from the book by Manfred Conte, or a longstanding script of Emeric's, *The Miracle in St Anthony's Lane*. After further indecision over the next Archers project, the Powell and Pressburger partnership came to an end.

Michael later insisted that there had been no big breakup, no argument; just a 'sad drifting apart', while Christopher Challis agrees that they 'had just reached a point where they wanted to do different things… but they were still very close friends. They didn't break up in that sense, and I think it's a great sadness that they didn't get back together'.

Evidence suggests however that the duo had simply run out of ideas. The Archers had not filmed a wholly original story since *A Matter of Life and Death* in 1946 – *The Red Shoes,* filmed in 1948, was already ten years old by that time. Certainly *River Plate* and *Ill Met by Moonlight* seemed unlikely subjects for the makers of *The Life and Death of Colonel Blimp* and *A Canterbury Tale*, containing little of the wit and eccentricity which had marked their best work. Few of their regular actors had featured in these two films and – perhaps most crucially – there were no roles for women such as Deborah Kerr, Pamela Brown or Kathleen Byron who had contributed so much to The Archers' success.

After a period spent living in Austria, Emeric Pressburger retreated to his home at Shoemaker's Cottage, with his remaining screen credits confined to that of writer/producer on *Miracle in Soho* in 1957 – the *Miracle in St Anthony's Lane* once considered as a possible Archers production – and a couple of screenplays under the pseudonym of Richard Imrie. Though seldom giving interviews, in 1971 Emeric spoke of the Archers partnership to Kevin Gough-Yates:

When we parted, Michael said to me, 'Well I want to tell you that I often did things when I didn't understand what you meant by them but I just did them blindly and they were all right most of the time'. Now this comes about not only because one trusts one's partner very much but also because… there was an inner response like a violin that would respond to an outside sound if it is tuned in a similar way; that must have been the case.

4

Alone again

Three full years after the breakup of The Archers, Michael Powell resurfaced with *Luna de Miel*, a barely disguised travelogue co-produced by himself and Césareo Gonsález. Powell also contributed to the screenplay with Luis Escobar, with other credits going to cameraman Georges Périnal – 20 years after *The Thief of Bagdad* – and Sir Thomas Beecham as conductor of the Mikis Theodorakis-composed ballet score.

Originally planned to star Paul Scofield and Moira Shearer, *Luna de Miel* was screened at the 1959 Cannes Festival as a Spanish entry where it was awarded the Special Prize of Commission Supérieure Technique before being shelved, with the suggestion that the Technirama production was being converted to an even wider screen process. Released unaltered in France in March 1961, the film finally reached Britain (as *Honeymoon*) a year later, when it had been cut from 109 minutes to 90.

With such a chequered distribution history, the film inevitably was not a box office success, and was not seen in England in its full version for many years. More seriously, this thoroughly disappointing picture did little to inspire confidence in Powell's future career without Pressburger. True, the theme of ballet and art taking precedence is here displayed once more, but the stiff acting failed to inject any passion into the inconsequential plot which was padded with endless shots of Spanish landscapes.

Mikis Theodorakis' theme, with added lyrics, became a schmaltzy hit in 1959 for the extraordinarily named Marino Marini and his Quartet as 'The Honeymoon Song'. The song was even performed by The Beatles in the early 1960s, and this latter version appeared on the *Live at the BBC* album released in 1994.

Leslie Halliwell called *Honeymoon* 'an incredibly shapeless travel poster... and... An unbelievable disaster from the co-creator of *The Red Shoes*', a judgement with which few – even Michael Powell himself – would disagree. Keen to make a successful follow-up, Micky settled on *The Reason Why* – Cecil Woodham-Smith's story of the Charge of the Light Brigade, with Rex Harrison and James Mason, only for the project to fold when screenwriter John Whiting died. To replace this, Michael began pre-production work on *The Loving Eye* by William Sansom, to be filmed in and around Powell's Kensington home and again intended to feature Paul Scofield and Moira Shearer, both presumably relieved at having escaped the dreadful *Honeymoon*. Unable to raise the necessary £150,000 to set the project rolling, he turned instead to a new original story by Leo Marks, former Head of Coding in the British Secret Service.

Marks had first become involved with Michael Powell over a projected spy story that was later abandoned. With another film on Freud also shelved, Marks now suggested, 'How would you like to make a film about a young man who kills people with his camera?' to which Powell immediately replied 'You're on!' Quickly in production at Pinewood and on location around London including the Melbury Road area where Powell had lived for many years, the picture was completed in five weeks – about half the average time. Financed came from Anglo-Amalgamated at a total cost of around £130,000, as the company sought to emulate the success of Hammer Films' low-budget horror productions.

Powell later said that the film was 'not about a diabolical murderer – it's about a cameraman'. To play Mark, Powell first approached Dirk Bogarde who, despite the uneven reception afforded *Ill Met by Moonlight*, had 'always hoped to work with Powell again'. Nevertheless, after reading the script, the actor 'refused to play in *Peeping Tom* which irritated Micky a little, so that we lost touch for a time [until] I was invited to present his Lifetime Achievement Award at the Cannes Festival and we had an extremely happy time together'.

Laurence Harvey was next choice – 'He would have completely resembled what we call a "focus puller"' – but was unavailable, and Powell finally settled on young German actor Carl Boehm. The character was to be an attractive, apparently normal young man, 'a figure to disturb an audience by asking to be identified with', Powell told *The Times*. 'My wife's criticism was that he was in fact not ordinary *enough* to achieve this… I think she may be right'.

Powell later described *Peeping Tom* as 'a very tender film… almost a romantic film'. The general consensus of opinion, however, did not agree, with the most extreme reaction that of Derek Hill in *Tribune* who fumed, 'The only really satisfactory way to dispose of [the film] would be to shovel it up and flush it swiftly down the nearest sewer'. Other reviews were scarcely less damaging. Anna Massey made one of her first screen appearances in the film and recalls its reception. 'I don't think we were completely surprised. It was a fairly disturbing and gruesome tale, and those types of film do tend to have a strong reaction'.

Although her father had appeared for Powell in a couple of pictures, Anna Massey did not know the director. 'He must have seen me somewhere, and just wanted me in the film', she says, recalling that Powell was 'quite fearsome in a way. He had the ability to make you feel quite uncomfortable sometimes, but he was somebody who believed in excellence, and he created a very tense atmosphere in order to tell that story'.

Later working with Alfred Hitchcock on *Frenzy* (1972), Miss Massey compares the two directors: 'Both created quite specific atmospheres, and both rehearsed a lot and didn't do very many takes. You couldn't relax, but if you think of the narrative of both films they weren't relaxing tales. They were tales of terror, and they [Powell and Hitchcock] were such masters that they knew

● Anna Massey and Carl Boehm in *Peeping Tom*.

the atmosphere that had to be on set before they turned'.

For Mrs Stephens, the blind mother, Pamela Brown was an early choice – 'She and Anna Massey could easily be mother and daughter', said Powell later. 'They look a bit like each other and have almost the same colour hair'. With Miss Brown unavailable, Maxine Audley took over, a little warily at first, having heard tales of Powell's now infamous behaviour on set. 'One actor', she says,

who will remain nameless for reasons of simple kindness, was desperately broke and begged Micky for a job...When the actor arrived.. Micky neglected to tell [him] that, for maximum surreal effect, he had placed him on a three foot square podium about thirty feet off the ground...Worse, Micky KNEW the actor suffered from vertigo, but that he didn't have enough money for next week's rent.

Fearing the worst, Miss Audley nevertheless recalls that '[his] conduct and behaviour throughout... was impeccable... Over the occasional post shoot drink, it was "Maxine" – but, on the studio floor, it was always a decorous "Miss Audley"'. Rehearsed for the first time as the blind mother, Powell told the actress 'You look as blind as a tree stump. I've nothing to show you'; the sum of his direction to her consisting of 'Just go on doing what you're doing... Be strong, frightened, blind and intuitive... which is what you are! Pity to waste those eyes – but, of course, they're not wasted, are they?' As the

killer's first victim, however, Brenda Bruce received rather less attention. 'I was cast by the casting office, arrived at the studio too shy to talk to anyone, did my scene several times, was thanked by Michael Powell and was home for tea!'

Powell explained to *The Times* that the film had come about simply because, of all those projects which he had prepared, 'this was the one the companies wanted to finance, so I made it first... I tried to go beyond the ordinary horror film of unexplained monsters, and instead to show why one human being should behave in this extraordinary way – it's a story of a human being first and foremost'. Some years later he would call it 'the most sincere of my films', but on release, *Peeping Tom* received an astounding amount of abuse from critics, with *The Times* virtually alone in not condemning the film. Criticisms flew over various aspects of the film, including the use of Powell's son Columba in the convincingly-filmed 'home movie' sequences. Again, Powell told *The Times*: 'My son understood what we were doing – I explained it all to him – and enjoyed joining in... I felt it gave the whole thing greater truth than if we had a routine child actor'.

More than 20 years later, Powell told *Films and Filming* that he was still 'very surprised because they weren't just bad reviews but vicious attacks'. The general tone of reviews suggested that the director 'was morbid and diseased in my mind and was trying to influence other people to be the same. I don't think any director had a worse attack'.

Faced with such a hostile reception, Anglo-Amalgamated panicked and, according to Powell, 'yanked the film... cancelled the British distribution, and sold the negative as soon as they could to an obscure black-marketeer of films who tried to forget it'. By the time of its US release exactly two years later, *Peeping Tom* had been cut from 109 minutes to 86, with European-released versions also suffering cuts. 'I was terribly surprised', said Powell. 'I had no idea that people were so innocent and puritan and inhibited as they were then'.

Maxine Audley felt that 'The whole point is that Micky meant it to be a kind of black comedy – and the furore it caused we all thought was Storm in a Teacup country'. As a footnote, she recalls hearing from a young cousin living in Berlin, where a screening of *Peeping Tom* at a Powell-Pressburger film festival 'was greeted with ecstasy by my cousin's students and, when she shyly acknowledged her relationship with me, she was briefly turned into an icon and, it seems, I was a Cult Star in Berlin – for about seven minutes!'

A 1976 French rerelease led the *International Herald Tribune* to report that the 'French laurels for *Peeping Tom* come late but they are richly deserved. A more gripping melodrama has not been projected on Parisian screens in a long time'. This began the long process of the film's revival, helped by Martin Scorsese's distribution of a full-length print in America. Scorsese suggests

● **Maxine Audley as the blind mother in *Peeping Tom* – 'the best role I've ever had in about seventy-five movies'.**

that it is the attention to lurid detail in *Peeping Tom* which caused such outrage – the depiction of the pornography trade and the seedier side of life presented truthfully and not merely for shock effect. Dilys Powell in *The Sunday Times* had offered the view that 'one would not be so disagreeably affected by this exercise... were it handled in a more bluntly debased fashion'. Michael Powell, she felt, was 'a director of skill and sensibility; the director whose daring and inquisitive eye gave us the superb *camera obscura* sequence... in *A Matter of Life of Death*'. Reflecting on Powell's career as a whole, however, she recalled the perverse 'vulgarity' of *A Canterbury Tale*'s 'glueman' and concluded that his descent into such an unpleasant area was not, after all, so surprising. Today, critical opinion on the film has reversed and *Peeping Tom* is now probably overpraised by many as Powell's 'masterpiece'. Certainly the film stands alone in Powell's work – and in British cinema. Only *Psycho* – released the same year – is in any way comparable yet while Hitchcock's picture won four Oscar nominations including Best Director, the reverberations from *Peeping Tom* were to have far-reaching consequences for Michael Powell – an absurd situation to be caused by a single film which is neither the director's best work nor his worst.

Immediately upon completion of *Peeping Tom,* Michael began work on *The Queen's Guards*, promising that it would not be 'an animated recruiting poster – in fact its irreverence will probably annoy the Army intensely when it's finished'. In fact the finished film provoked little more than indifference in most quarters, and Michael's final opinion was that it was 'the most inept piece of film-making that I have ever produced or directed'.

A strangely unmoving story, *The Queen's Guards* left reviewers perplexed, with *The Times* remarking that 'Ever since *The Edge of the World*, [Powell] has been unpredictable, and that is by no means a necessarily bad thing' although they felt that '[he] has never quite fulfilled his tantalizing promise'.

When preparing *The Edge of the World* in 1937, Powell had considered casting real-life father and son Malcolm and Geoffrey Keen as father and son in that film. More than 20 years later he achieved this with Raymond and Daniel Massey in *The Queen's Guards*, but later reflected 'that a father and son are about the last parts that a father and son would want to play'. 'Mickey (*sic*) may be right', says Daniel Massey, who continues, 'I had been in the guards on National Service, while my father had served in the Canadian Army in World War One. But father had a heavy American accent [in the film] playing an ex or old and retired guards officer, and I thought the premise incongruous for that reason and I never really settled to it'.

Daniel Massey also witnessed further examples of Powell's imperfect behaviour on set. 'I did not respect his bullying tactics with certain actors', he says, feeling that 'this impulse was unpredictable and never helpful to the quality of the film'. Nevertheless, the actor 'will always remember the experience of working with Mickey (*sic*). It was rewarding. You learned. He was a sort of genius, no question about that', although he thought *The Queen's*

Guards ultimately 'uneven but like all his work it had flashes of brilliance'.

An unquestionable lesser achievement in Powell's career, *The Queen's Guards* was mystifyingly hailed by American film historian William K. Everson as 'Powell's equivalent to John Ford's *The Man who shot Liberty Valance*' with an 'appeal… more to the emotions than to the intellect, and perhaps it is still a little too early for it to appreciated in England'. *Peeping Tom*, he continued, had 'anticipated audience fashions… by too great a margin, while *The Queen's Guards* offered respect for the past… when others were preaching anger and revolt. Time has already vindicated *Peeping Tom*, and will surely do the same for *The Queen's Guards*'. Powell merely labelled the picture 'a big yawn'.

With the continued hostility of much of the press – and even sections of the film industry itself – the *Peeping Tom* 'scandal' virtually ended Powell's career in Britain. 'It did me a lot of harm professionally', he later said. 'It meant that any subject I wanted to do which was unusual… I could not raise the money'. This put paid to possible movies of *The Battle of April Storm* featuring Richard Burton but which was rejected by United Artists, and Graham Greene's *The Living Room* starring Rex Harrison, Samantha Eggar and Pamela Brown. Bryan Forbes recalls: 'To my great regret', he says, 'when I was Head of Production at EMI [Michael] brought me *The Living Room* which he was anxious to make and which I would have made, but I was overruled by my board who did not think it had sufficient commercial possibilities. How they determined this before a single foot of film was exposed remains a mystery'.

Forbes 'would have loved to have included him in my programme and thus repaid him for the kindnesses he had extended to me at the start of my own career… we shamefully neglect such talents in this country and he was a major talent'.

Frozen out of British feature film work, Powell's reputation as a director had never been so low. In 1963, American producer Herbert Brodkin asked him to direct two episodes of his short-lived (24 episodes) *Espionage* series for British television, described in Leslie Halliwell's *Teleguide* as 'somewhat gloomy but well made… with excellent guest stars'. For *Never turn your Back on a Friend* and *A Free Agent*, Powell called in Pamela Brown, Anthony Quayle, writer Leo Marks, and cameraman Geoffrey Faithfull, who had photographed many of Powell's early British features and 'quota quickies'. With little likelihood of further work in the UK, Powell was contacted again by Hein Heckroth, now working with the Frankfurt Opera, and agreed to direct a one-hour film of Bartok's opera *Bluebeard's Castle* in Zagreb to be produced and financed by singer Norman Foster. Another 'composed' film with a pre-recorded music score, it remains unreleased in Britain, although Jenny Laird recalls a screening at London's Everyman Cinema. 'This struck me as a sad film – full of, as I thought, the sadness of evil', she says. 'I wrote [Michael Powell] a note saying so and he replied yes, it was sad, but not evil. Evilness is not sad – "Evil men enjoy it"'.

Powell worked in America for the first time in 1965, routinely directing two more television episodes for Herbert Brodkin: one each of *The Defenders* – a popular, long running series (132 episodes) about a father-and-son lawyer team – and *The Nurses* (also known as *The Doctors and the Nurses*), which followed the trusted formula of depicting life in a large hospital, with 103 episodes filmed between 1962 and 1965. Both series were filmed in black and white.

These projects however, barely kept the director occupied as he now drifted professionally. 1966 found him 'down under' bringing popular Australian novel *They're a Weird Mob* to the screen.

A bestseller in its native country, the book was virtually unknown elsewhere until Gregory Peck bought a screen option, intending to produce an 'Ealing-style' comedy aimed at 'winning a medal at the Cannes Film Festival'. When the star's American backers rejected the idea, the option was dropped and immediately taken up by Michael Powell.

Powell met the author, who insisted that 'the Australian characters would not be permitted to speak like Cockneys', and a screenplay was written first by Powell, then by O'Grady – neither of them filmable – while a financing deal was hammered out largely by Googie Withers' husband John McCallum, Chairman of Williamson Theatres in Australia. A modest budget would be split between Australian sources, the National Film Finance Corporation in

● **Co-producers James Mason and Michael Powell in Australia for *Age of Consent*.**

London and the Rank Organisation who would distribute the picture in Britain. All seemed set, yet it took another three years – 'John Davis couldn't make up his mind', said Powell – before filming began in October 1965, with a completely new script written by Richard Imrie, the pseudonym of none other than Emeric Pressburger.

According to John McCallum, 'The film broke all box-office records in Australia, grossing between two and three million dollars'. Euphoria was short-lived however when 'the full financial statements came in... The distributors took a 35 per cent fee, and this, together with extremely high theatre and publicity costs – deducted before the producer got a penny – meant that it took us eight years before we recouped production costs, let alone made a profit'.

Powell claimed that, after British critics had 'received [the film] in dead silence', John Davis presented it as a second feature with little promotion. As Gregory Peck and his backers had predicted, the story attracted little interest outside Australia. Nevertheless, Powell enjoyed his time 'down under', and the success of *They're a Weird Mob* in its home country is credited by many as the first step in the recovery of Australian cinema, which led to later internationally acclaimed films like *Picnic at Hanging Rock* and *Breaker Morant*.

Returning to London, Powell co-produced (with Herbert Brodkin) another Leo Marks story, *Sebastian*, an espionage drama based on a team of codebreakers working for the Secret Service.

It seems likely that Powell originally intended to direct *Sebastian*, but after control shifted away from him during pre-production the job eventually went to David Greene, whose only previous film had been a version of H.P. Lovecraft's *The Shuttered Room* (1966). Greene would later work in American television, with his biggest success as co-director of the 1976 series *Rich Man, Poor Man*.

Filmed in England, *Sebastian* contained some innovative ideas by Marks but was otherwise no more than a competently-made spy thriller, complete with the obligatory (for 1967) psychedelic sequence. The presence of Dirk Bogarde – who replaced Rex Harrison – ensured the film a popular audience, with other big names in the cast including John Gielgud, Lilli Palmer and the promising young Susannah York. *Variety* praised direction, acting and dialogue but thought 'a fatal flaw in basic plotting', left the production only 'moderately entertaining'.

Twenty-four years after a failure to agree terms on *I Know Where I'm Going!*, Michael Powell and James Mason came together on the other side of the world to co-produce *Age of Consent* on location in Australia, with Powell's son Kevin as Production Manager. The film was completed quickly and without major difficulties, although on release there were minor problems with the British censor, who removed the opening bedroom scene between Mason and Clarissa Kaye, here meeting for the first time and married a few years later.

Reviews were mixed, with some critics accepting the amiable intent of the picture, while others – perhaps expecting more serious subject matter from the two producers – considered it a let-down. Most comment was reserved for the amount of nudity ('a painter's nudity', said Powell) in the film – the deleted opening, and a later swimming scene with Helen Mirren. James Mason 'had nursed a secret hope that we might break through the reluctance in British and US markets to accept films made in Australia', but felt that 'Michael and I were persuaded to cut certain passages from the film' in order to avoid 'the difficult and (in this case) unsuitable "X" certificate'. Distributors, however, then released *Age of Consent* 'in tandem with another film… selected by the salesmen of Columbia on the Rank circuit [which] flaunted an "X", believe it or not'. Powell recalled what he considered

one of the best scenes I've ever made in which a dog puts on its own collar. He was a wonderful dog called Geoffrey, and he had a real old sergeant major owner and a quality I can only describe as cunning. So when I told him that I wanted the dog to put on his own collar he said, 'I'll have a word with him sir'. I kept hoping people would remember the film and say 'That's the one in which the dog puts on his own collar' – but they never did.

With less than enthusiastic reviews of all of his 1960s work so far, a further reunion with Emeric Pressburger seemed a distinct – and welcome – possibility when the two collaborated on Michael Frayn's *The Russian Interpreter,* until first Peter Sellers rejected Powell as director and then Frayn objected to Pressburger's ideas for the screenplay. Emeric quietly retired to his cottage again as Powell doggedly pursued backing for one more directing job.

The 1970s were to be a frustrating decade, with yet more unrealized projects, most notable among them being a version of Shakespeare's *The Tempest* – 'a sort of surrealist *Tempest*' – starring James Mason and Mia Farrow. First announced in 1970, the project seemed at last to be making progress when, in May 1975, Powell announced, 'I've got all the cast together (Topol, Frankie Howerd, Malcolm McDowell), all the letters of intent and nearly all the money'. Even with a complete screenplay (by Powell) and an enthusiastic backer in Frixos Constantine, the spectre of *Peeping Tom* still haunted Powell's reputation. After Constantine, seeking support for pre-production costs, was bluntly informed that 'Rank did not intend to work with Michael Powell again', the project was again left to gather dust.

Also in 1975, Powell's first and only novel, *A Waiting Game* was published, but remained unadapted. Film work eventually came his way from an apparently unlikely source.

Founded by J. Arthur Rank in 1951 as a unit making films for Saturday matinees, the Children's Film Foundation turned out short features for this purpose which were rarely seen elsewhere. During 1972, Michael Powell was a member of the CFF board and proposed filming an original children's story by Emeric Pressburger. The modest film was photographed by Christopher Challis, bringing an expertise previously unseen in such a production. *The Boy who turned Yellow* was the first CFF film to use the new Panavision camera and lenses.

The result was hardly a 'new Archers' film, nor to any real extent a true Powell-Pressburger collaboration. It was filmed at Shepperton Studios, with ten days' location work at Hampstead, Holborn Tube Station and the Tower of London itself, where the governor allowed the crew every co-operation in shooting – even during the busy Easter tourist season.

The major problem facing the production – apart from the 'terribly low budget' – was the 'yellowing' of the scene on the tube train. Christopher Challis explains: 'It was a clever original story by Emeric, but you can't technically turn things yellow with filters'. The solution was yellow costumes, wigs and make-up and even painting the inside and outside of a London tube train! Although Powell later claimed that John Davis had attempted to prevent its release, the film won the Children's Film Foundation prize – the 'Chiffy' – voted for by the children themselves.

Fittingly, as the last complete film to be directed by Michael Powell, *The Boy who turned Yellow* featured Esmond Knight making his tenth appearance for the director and playfully demanding, 'When are you going to give me a decent role?'

While all assumed Knight's career was ended in 1941 following the loss of his sight, Esmond had received a telephone call from Powell asking 'When are you going to come back to work?' Since then, Knight had made several appearances for The Archers and been seen in many other films including *Uncle Silas, Holiday Camp, Halfway House, The River* and Laurence Olivier's Shakespearean trilogy *Hamlet, Henry V* and *Richard III*. Ironically, he also took a role in *Sink the Bismarck* (1960) – the story of the ship whose attack had blinded him.

Esmond Knight continued to work into his eighties, collapsing from heart failure while filming in Spain in February 1987. Michael Powell wrote of his longtime friend, 'That gallant heart no longer beats… If he had not been blinded in the war with Hitler, we would all know his name today, and would have said to one another, "A great actor is dead"'.

A follow-up to *The Boy who Turned Yellow*, *The Magic Umbrella* – again from a story by Pressburger – was rejected by the Foundation, due, Powell claimed, to the opposition of old foe John Davis.

With no new movies, even The Archers' classic films were disappearing from view, with only cut versions and substandard prints available for screening. In America, several of their films had never even been seen in their original state. Assisted by the BBC, the National Film Archive assembled and restored a full-length print of *Colonel Blimp* in 1978, followed by *A Canterbury Tale*, which did much to boost the reputation of that film and its makers.

That same year (1978), saw Michael Powell's final completed work, a return almost to where his career as a major film director had begun.

Made for BBC Television, *Return to the Edge of the World* opens with Powell newly filmed at Pinewood Studios where he recalls his beginnings in cinema before leading the surviving cast members from *Edge of the World* back to the island which had meant so much to them 40 years before. Sadly, Niall MacGinnis had died shortly before filming began; Finlay Currie had died some years before, while both Eric Berry and Belle Chrystall were unable to make the trip. That left Michael Powell himself, John Laurie, Grant (Hamish) Sutherland and Sydney Streeter. Of the Foula islanders of 1936, only six remained although those same families were represented by their descendants.

John Laurie became our guide of the island during the newly-filmed sequences. Best known for his role in the long running (1967-77) television comedy series *Dad's Army*, he had already been a familiar screen personality for almost 50 years, following a stage career in which he was one of the youngest actors ever to play *Hamlet* at Stratford. Hitchcock's *The Thirty Nine Steps* (1935) established him as a 'name' actor after a couple of 'quickies' for Michael Powell, and he was soon one of the best-known faces in British cinema. *Return to the Edge of the World* was his final film appearance before his death in 1980.

On a rain swept island, Laurie, Sutherland and Powell movingly evoked the spirit of that long-ago expedition and the dedication of those who took part. The 61-minute *Edge of the World* was sandwiched between the newly filmed colour material until the NFA produced a new print featuring the full-length version running at 85 minutes. Shown at the 1990 London Film Festival, it was later released on home video.

The 1980s opened on a promising note when a special BAFTA Award was presented to both Michael Powell and Emeric Pressburger by Deborah Kerr, who rightly described the recognition as long overdue. A Cannes Lifetime Award went to Powell, and he and Emeric were among the first to receive the Fellowship of the British Film Institute in 1983. Despite this apparent recognition of their vast contribution to British cinema, there remained no new offers of work for either Powell or Pressburger.

5

Iris out

Again frustrated at home, Powell headed back to America where his earlier works were now beginning to be appreciated by a 'new wave' of directors. A term as lecturer at Dartmouth College kept him active as his reputation spread, partly due to Martin Scorsese's championing of *Peeping Tom* and *The Tales of Hoffmann*. Francis Ford Coppola declared himself an admirer and, more practically, offered the 75-year-old Powell a position at his newly-formed Zoetrope Studios, the only serious independent film studios in Hollywood at the time. Creating a post of 'Senior Director in Residence', Coppola looked to the veteran director for guidance. 'My advice is asked. It doesn't have to be taken', Powell said. 'Scripts are written. I read them and give my opinion. There's a good deal to do. I'm pretty busy. I find it's busier advising than making a film!'

There was also the possiblity of a new Michael Powell movie – he had brought with him at least one possibility in a film of Pavlova's life which he had been discussing with cameraman Erwin Hillier since the late 1970s. 'I liked the idea', Powell told the *Glasgow Herald*, 'because, having made one or two outstanding dance films, I thought [it] would fill in every dance fan's knowledge of the past sixty to eighty years'. Powell was preparing a script with a Russian writer at Mosfilm studios on this first UK/USSR production when Moldavian director Emil Louteanau was assigned to the project and insisted on writing his own screenplay.

Finally credited only as production co-ordinator for the Western version of *Pavlova – A Woman For All Time* – 'a big romantic film of the kind I couldn't make' – Powell's active participation was confined to the casting of three British actors – James Fox, Roy Kinnear and Bruce Forsyth – and the supervision of dubbing the picture into English in London. Present for the editing, Powell said 'The picture was long – I might say it was too long. Thelma and I went to Russia for four months and the director was quite co-operative, but all directors hate to cut their film'.

Firmly installed at Zoetrope, Micky finally and reluctantly abandoned *The Tempest* and turned to Ursula Le Guin's *Earthsea Trilogy*. Impressed and intrigued by the first of the books, *A Wizard of Earthsea* published ten years earlier, Powell began a correspondence with the author which continued through the next two volumes in the series. Although they had never met, he suggested the books be filmed. 'I was dead set against it', says Ursula Le Guin, 'until he sent me ten or fifteen pages, handwritten in his magnificent black scrawl, of the beginning of a draft script. It was irresistible, and I said "OK, but we have to work on this together." He said "That's exactly what I wanted!"' Work continued, largely by mail, although Powell and Le Guin finally met on two occasions in America.

'When we had it to our satisfaction', she says, 'we took it to Hollywood and showed it around a bit – we didn't get far. Michael was old enough that they were afraid they couldn't get insurance. We were not going to let anybody else direct it, although we would have accepted a co-director'.

Powell was well aware of the problems connected with insurance at the age of 76. 'I'll suggest that the project goes ahead – and I hold the director's hand', he said, but the insistence of the two writers that 'We weren't offering the script as a sketch for them to fiddle with, but as a fairly finished thing' found no favour with executives, and *Earthsea* remained no more than a five-minute film made by Powell and his students at Dartmouth College during his residence there.

At this period in his life, Powell seemed finally to have mellowed from the often abrasive personality of his earlier days. Le Guin reckons that 'working with Michael on the screenplay was one of the greatest pleasures of my writing life. His passion, imagination, wit and vitality were marvellous; his good nature was inexhaustible. I loved to see him *thinking in film;* sometimes he would hold up his hands making a camera-sight of them, and look through it to frame the scene he was seeing in his mind's eyes'. Maxine Audley, too, confirms that he had become 'hugely congenial – a man with a load of mischief. Nearly giggly', and although Stewart Granger confirms that Powell 'still had those piercing brilliant blue eyes' which had struck such terror into many an actor during the 1930s and 1940s, Ursula Le Guin was left feeling that 'Michael was proof, if needed, that the real thing, the genuine genius, can be a loveable, admirable, complete, and fascinating human being. He had plenty of ego but none of it was competitive or destructive in my experience… he was a perfect person to *work with,* which is very high praise in my mind'.

With the failure of the *Earthsea* project, followed almost immediately by the collapse of Zoetrope Studios, Powell published the first volume of his autobiography, begun in Hollywood four years earlier. *A Life in Movies* told of the first 43 years of his life, covering virtually the entire history of motion pictures as an entertainment and art form. Few could have covered those years with such authority, from Silents to Sound to Colour, as the three parts of the book were entitled. Although a bestseller, and winner of the British Film Institute Book Award, there were some who felt that it took liberties with the past. Moira Shearer describes *A Life in Movies* as 'an extraordinary piece of semi-fiction'.

Perhaps with age his memory was faulty or his love of fantasy overwhelmed any strict adherence to truth. Whatever the reason, there are, in this book, amazing 'verbatim' conversations from forty or fifty years ago and descriptions of events which simply never took place. In this process he maligns many people, both the living and the dead, and it is a deeply unattractive last word from a man of talent and achievement.

In February 1988, Emeric Pressburger died at the age of 86. Of his long-time friend, Michael Powell wrote in *The Observer*:

- **'I loved to see him thinking in film – holding his hands up to make a camera sight, to frame the scene he was seeing in his mind's eye'. (Ursula Le Guin)**

● Powell in 1986, promoting his first volume of autobiography, *A Life in Movies*, and still proudly identified with The Archers logo.

For what he meant to me, I look to O. Henry: 'I thought that I had found an original theme for my novel, and then I became aware that [he] had been there before me. But instead of writing a whole book, he had put it in one line: "but can them that helps others, help themselves?" The answer is – they can't without a partner whom they love and trust. And that is what Imre Pressburger has meant to me. They tell me he died in his sleep, but I am sure it was in the middle of a joke.

Apart from those few screenplays Emeric had produced since the breakup of The Archers, there had also been two novels – *Killing a Mouse on Sunday*, published in 1961 and filmed in 1964 by Fred Zinnemann as *Behold a Pale Horse* (Pressburger had no involvement with the screen version) and 1966's *The Glass Pearls*. Perhaps alongside another unpublished novel and a few unproduced scripts and outlines lies an incomplete draft of a long-rumoured autobiography, said to be under way at the same time as *A Life in Movies* but as yet unpublished.

Always the less flamboyant member of the partnership – 'a kindly and silent figure' according to Jenny Laird – Pressburger's contribution to The Archers partnership had always been in danger of being overlooked. Daniel Massey pays this tribute to the writer: 'I felt that the light rather went out of his [Powell's] working life when he and Emeric parted. Mickey (*sic*) was wonderful visually with the camera – he could tell a good story wonderfully well – but he had no real touch for the written word. Emeric did. He was a master. That's the tale, in my view'. Moira Shearer, too, considered Pressburger 'very necessary to the success of the Archers. He was a most charming and delightful friend with whom I kept in touch until the end of his life'.

Michael Powell had of course always been eager to acknowledge his partner's contribution to that startling run of successful movies The Archers had turned out during the 1940s. 'They were all written by this little man, with the big head, and big, beautiful observant eyes', he wrote. 'He has been honoured by his profession at home and abroad, and ignored by the English Establishment'. Powell, too, had been consistently overlooked by that same establishment, claiming that during the *Colonel Blimp* controversy in 1943 a Minister had warned him 'the Old Man (Churchill) will be very cross and you'll never get a knighthood'. So it proved to be. While Carol Reed, David Lean, Richard Attenborough and Alfred Hitchcock – an American citizen since 1950 – all received knighthoods, both Powell and Pressburger were conspicuously absent from all honours lists throughout their lives. 'And that is as it should be', observed Powell at one point. 'Too much hobnobbing with the great and powerful is bad for an artist'. Similarly, the want of backing for a new film was philosophically summarized as 'just the way of it', although, recalling his early benefactors Harry Lachman, Jerry Jackson and Joe Rock – all Americans – he reflected 'The English haven't helped me whenever I've really needed them'.

Of more satisfaction was the continuing restoration and critical and public acclaim of Powell and Pressburger's earlier works. Apart from the acclaimed reissue of *The Life and Death of Colonel Blimp* and the two-week Archers retrospective in New York, *Gone to Earth* was now being seen in its original version for the first time in 25 years, showcased at the London Film Festival, while a reissue of *Black Narcissus* ran at London's Electric Cinema for three months in early 1986.

Despite this, there would be no new Michael Powell movie during the 1980s, a decade he divided between his Gloucestershire cottage, an apartment off Broadway and the offices of 'Michael Powell Productions' (which retained the archery target as its logo) in New York. An intriguing possiblity was raised in 1988 when the Golan brothers – owners of the Cannon Group – were reported to be financing Powell's production of Edgar Allan Poe's *The Fall of the House of Usher*. At other times backing was rumoured to be coming from Coppola and Scorsese, but Powell told *The Observer* 'I am trying to make up my mind whether to make one last film or finish my book' – the second volume of his memoirs,

● **Archer to the end: Michael Powell's company notepaper in 1989, 30 years after The Archers had split up.**

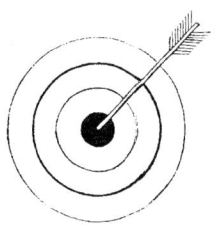 MICHAEL POWELL PRODUCTIONS

taking up where *A Life in Movies* left off. 'I think the book is more important, but there isn't time for both', he said. 'So long as I can set it all down… I will have done a complete job'.

In France in 1927 at the age of 21 Michael Powell had married an American dancer whose name he did not even feel it necessary to reveal in his autobiography. Three weeks later they separated permanently and in July 1943 he married former model Frankie Reidy – seen in the opening sequence of *The Edge of the World*. Two sons were born: Kevin in August 1945 on the day shooting began on *A Matter of Life and Death,* and Columba – the young boy in the 'home movies' of *Peeping Tom* – eight years later.

By the early 1970s the couple were living apart, Powell now sharing a cottage in Avening which he had bought with long-time favourite actress Pamela Brown, the culmination of a relationship which had lasted almost 30 years. By the middle of the decade, Pamela's always frail health finally gave out and she died at the cottage in September 1975. Powell and Frankie had never divorced, however, and she agreed to appear in the 1978 *Return to the Edge of the World,* although her scenes were filmed in London and intercut with the location footage. In 1983, she died following a stroke only a matter of days after their fortieth wedding anniversary.

A year later, aged 78, Michael married Martin Scorsese's film editor Thelma Schoonmaker, an Academy Award winner for her work on *Raging Bull* who was to complete the second volume of Michael Powell's autobiographical memoirs, *Million Dollar Movie*. This had reached only the first draft stage when Michael, who had been suffering from cancer for some time, returned to England on a private plane chartered by Warner Brothers and, shortly after, died at his home in Lee Cottages at 2.30 on the afternoon of 19 February 1990.

Powell once told an interviewer 'I *live* cinema', and to the end he remained loyal to that spirit. Obituary notices in the English press requested, in place of flowers, donations to the National Film Archive. The BFI issued a press release acknowledging the unique relationship which had existed between themselves and the director, and in November of that year the 34th London Film Festival was 'Dedicated to the Memory of Michael Powell'.

Many tributes were paid in the days following his death. Most remarkably, for someone who had not made a film in 18 years, Powell was still regarded as a major influential figure in British movies. Gilbert Adair of *The Independent* said 'With his death the British cinema has lost the most indispensible of its creators', while in the same newspaper a few days later, Marius Goring wrote, 'Those who did not like working with him were probably unable to meet the standards he expected from them… He was a master craftsman of the camera… Working with Powell was one of the greatest experiences of my life'.

Million Dollar Movie – a book heavily preoccupied with Powell's own approaching death and that of Emeric Pressburger – was again held by many of those mentioned to be often a work of fantasy, but also revealed Powell's ulti-

mately thwarted long-standing desire to work in Hollywood. The studio-domi-
nated Hollywood of Powell's dreams, however, would never have supported a
film-maker of his independence. Like others before him, Powell would have
been no less frustrated by Hollywood's inflexibility than he had been by indifference in Britain. Although the studio system had broken down by the time
Powell finally did reach Hollywood in 1980, the business conglomerates which
took their place still resisted the efforts of any maverick independent film-
maker. Scorsese and Spielberg could justify and control their own projects only
as long as they made successful pictures, but Coppola found to his cost that a single flop – *One From the Heart* – could cause his cherished Zoetrope dream to
evaporate. Having been constantly at odds with Rank or Korda in Britain, what
chance would Powell have had up against the likes of Harry Cohn, Louis B.
Mayer or Jack Warner?

Instead, like Orson Welles, Powell spent many years struggling - and failing
– to raise backing for a new film as his past career was being acclaimed world-
wide, but unlike Welles, the nearest comparable independent film-maker in
America, he could not finance his own movies by appearing in those of other
people. New projects – *The House of Usher, The Earthsea Trilogy, The Tempest*, a new
story by Emeric, *The Russian Interpreter*, a film of *M Butterfly,* a biography of
Beethoven to be co-directed with Jack Cardiff – all in the end came to nothing
for the want of a modest budget while studio executives ploughed huge sums
into endless sequels and derivatives of past successes. Given the inferior quality
of Powell's later works, it may well be that some of these proposed movies may
ultimately have proven of only minor importance, but it must nevertheless be
deeply regretted that a film-maker of Michael Powell's vision and imagination
should spend virtually 20 years unable to complete a single film.

Christopher Challis, whose personal and professional relationship with
Powell stretched over more than 40 years, speaks of Powell as 'a complex person. I loved working with him because he was a sort of Boy Scout in some ways.
He had great qualities of leadership and the ability to make people believe in
what they were doing, even if in their innermost hearts they knew something
wasn't very good'.

Above all else, Powell believed in his movies, even to the exclusion of critical comment. He had never enjoyed an easy relationship with critics, unlike his
contemporary Alfred Hitchcock. 'I'm too exotic', he said. 'Too unpredictable
in results and choice of subject… I don't go after the same sort of story all the
time'. Christopher Challis agrees that both Powell and Pressburger 'desperately wanted to do their own sorts of films. That's what they set out to do, and they
cared about them very much'. That care is to be seen in every frame of their
best films.

Filmography

* Denotes a film for which there is no known print in existence and which is therefore officially considered 'lost'

MARE NOSTRUM
(1925) MGM.
Director: Rex Ingram; *Screenplay:* Willis Goldbeck from the novel by Vicente Blasco Ibanez
Cast: includes Alice Terry, Antonio Moreno. Powell as 'Grip, title designer'

THE MAGICIAN
(1926) MGM.
Director: Rex Ingram
Cast: includes Alice Terry, Paul Wegener, Ivan Petrovic, Firmin Gérmier, Gladys Hamer, Powell as 'Clown' (uncredited)

* THE GARDEN OF ALLAH
(1927) MGM.
Director: Rex Ingram; *Screenplay:* Willis Goldbeck, from the novel by Robert Hitchens
Cast: includes Alice Terry, Ivan Petrovic, Marcel Vibert, and Michael Powell as 'A Tourist'

TRAVELAUGHS
(1927-28).
An unspecified number of two-reel short fims produced/directed independently by Harry Lachman and featuring Michael Powell in various guises, probably also acting as co-writer, cameraman and co-director.

● Michael Powell, believe it or not, as star of one of the *Travelaughs* two-reelers around 1927/28.

CHAMPAGNE
(1928, 86 minutes) British International Pictures. Distributed by Wardour Films.
Director: Alfred Hitchcock; *Producer:* John Maxwell; *Screenplay:* Eliot Stannard, from a story by Walter Mycroft, adapted by Alfred Hitchcock; *Director of Photography:* Jack Cox; *Stills Photographer:* Michael Powell
Cast: includes Betty Balfour, Gordon Harker, Ferdinand von Alten, Jean Bradin, Jack Trevor

That was probably the lowest ebb in my output.
Alfred Hitchcock

THE MANXMAN

(1928, 91 minutes) British International Pictures. Distributed by Wardour Films.
Director: Alfred Hitchcock; *Producer:* John Maxwell; *Screenplay:* Eliot Stannard, from a
novel by Sir Hall Caine; *Director of Photography*: Jack Cox; *Film Editor:* Emile de Ruelle;
Stills Photographer: Michael Powell
Cast: includes Carl Brisson, Malcolm Keen, Anny Ondra, Randle Ayrton, Clare Greet

The only point of interest is that it was my last silent movie... a very banal picture.
Alfred Hitchcock

BLACKMAIL

(1929, 96 minutes) British International Pictures. Distributed by Wardour Films.
Director: Alfred Hitchcock; *Producer*: John Maxwell; *Screenplay*: Alfred Hitchcock, Charles
Bennett, Benn W. Levy, Garnett Weston (and Michael Powell, uncredited), from a play by
Charles Bennett; *Director of Photography:* Jack Cox
Cast: includes Anny Ondra, John Longden, Donald Calthrop, Cyril Ritchard, Sara Allgood,
Charles Paton, Hannah Jones, Phyllis Monkman, Johnny Butt, Percy Parsons, Sam Livesey

Most draggy. it has no speed or pace and very little suspense... In performance the standout is
Donald Calthrop as the rat crook. He looks it.
Variety

CASTE

(1930, 70 minutes) Harry Rowson. Distributed by United Artists.
Director: Campbell Gullan (and Michael Powell, uncredited); *Producer:* Jerome Jackson;
Screenplay: Michael Powell, from the play by T.W. Robertson
Cast: includes Sebastian Shaw, Nora Swinburne, Hermione Baddeley, Ben Field, Alan Napier,
Edward Chapman, Mabel Terry-Lewis

77 PARK LANE

(1931, 82 minutes) Famous Players' Guild. Distributed by United Artists.
Director: Albert de Courville; *Producer:* John Harding; *Screenplay*: Michael Powell and Reginald
Berkeley, from the play by Walter Hackett
Cast: includes Dennis Neilson-Terry, Betty Stockfield, Malcolm Keen, Esmond Knight, Molly
Johnson, Ben Welden, Cecil Humphreys, Roland Culver, John Turnbull, Percival Coyte, W.
Molesworth Blow

PERFECT UNDERSTANDING

(1932, 80 minutes) Gloria Swanson British Productions. Distributed by United
Artists.
Director: Cyril Gardner; *Producer:* Gloria Swanson; *Screenplay:* Miles Malleson, Michael Powell;
Photography: Curt Courant
Cast: includes Gloria Swanson, Laurence Olivier, Genevieve Tobin, Michael Farmer, John
Halliday, Nigel Playfair, Nora Swinburne, O.B. Clarence, Mary Jerrold

Dull and talky picture, done in the uninspiring British style.
Variety

* TWO CROWDED HOURS

(1931, 43 minutes) Film Engineering. Distributed by Fox (GB).
Director: Michael Powell; *Producers:* Jerome Jackson and Henry Cohen; *Screenplay:* J. Jefferson Farjeon (and Michael Powell, uncredited); *Photography:* Geoffrey Faithfull; *Film Editor:* John Seabourne; *Art Director:* C. Saunders
Cast: John Longden (Harry Fielding), Jane Walsh (Joyce Danton), Jerry Verno (Jim), Michael Hogen (Scammell), Edward Barber (Tom Murray)

Comedy drama about a murderer (Michael Hogan) out to gain revenge on those who gave evidence against him. Fielding rescues his fiancée Jane Walsh from Scammell, who is later killed in a car crash. A simple plot similar to Will Hay's last film *My Learned Friend* (Ealing, 1943).

* MY FRIEND THE KING

(1931, 47 minutes) Film Engineering. Distributed by Paramount (GB).
Director: Michael Powell; *Producer:* Jerome Jackson; *Screenplay:* J. Jefferson Farjeon, from his own story; *Photography:* Geoffrey Faithfull; *Film Editor:* John Seabourne; *Art Director:* C. Saunders
Cast: Jerry Verno (Jim), Robert Holmes (Captain Felz), Tracy Holmes (Count Huelin), Eric Pavitt (King Ludwig), Phyllis Loring (Princess Helma), Luli Hohenberg (Countess Zena), H. Saxon Snell (Karl), Victor Fairlie (Josef)

Comedy. Taxi driver Jim becomes involved in a plot to kidnap Ruritanian child king Ludwig and, masquerading as a countess, rescues the nine-year-old ruler from revolutionaries led by Count Huelin.

Jerry Verno, who scored such a decided comedy hit in Two Crowded Hours *as a taxi driver, continues his automobile career in this feature... There is not much sublety about the burlesque, but it is presented with plenty of action and pictorial effects... Not great stuff, this, but one that helps pass three quarters of an hour quite pleasantly.*
Picturegoer

RYNOX

(1931, 48 minutes) Film Engineering for Ideal Films. Distributed by Ideal.
Director: Michael Powell; *Producer:* Jerome Jackson; *Screenplay:* Jerome Jackson, Michael Powell and Philip Macdonald, from the novel by Philip Macdonald; *Photography:* Geoffrey Faithfull, Arthur Grant; *Film Editor:* John Seabourne; *Art Director:* G.C. Waygrove; *Sound Recording:* Rex Howarth
Cast: Stewart Rome (Boswell Marsh/F.X. Benedik), Dorothy Boyd (Peter), John Longden (Tony Benedik), Edward Willard (Captain James), Charles Paton, Leslie Mitchell (Woolrich), Sybil Grove (Secretary), Fletcher Lightfoot (Prout)

Drama. Claiming he has been threatened by mysterious stranger Boswell Marsh, the business tycoon F.X. Benedik is found murdered. Tony takes over the business and discovers that Marsh never existed but was created by Benedik Senior who intended to commit suicide after learning that he had only a year to live.

This unpretentious mystery picture has some claim to originality in conception... Rather complicated, but nevertheless quite clearly told. Moreover, it is not too easy to foresee the ending... Camera work is good and the action quite brisk.
Picturegoer

* THE RASP

(1931, 44 minutes) Film Engineering. Distributed by Fox (GB).

Director: Michael Powell; *Producer*: Jerome Jackson; *Screenplay*: Philip Macdonald, from his own story; *Photography*: Geoffrey Faithfull; *Art Director:* Frank Wells

Cast: Claude Horton (Anthony Gethryn), Phyllis Loring (Lucia Masterson), C.M. Hallard (Sir Arthur Coates), James Raglan (Alan Deacon), Thomas Weguelin (Inspector Boyd), Carol Coombe (Dora Masterson), Leonard Brett (Jimmy Masterson)

When Cabinet Minister John Hoode is murdered at his country house, his secretary, Alan Deacon is arrested by Inspector Boyd. Journalist Anthony Gethryn uncovers the real murderer – business rival Sir Arthur Coates. Deacon is reunited with his fiancée, Dora Masterson and Gethryn proposes to Dora's sister Lucia.

* THE STAR REPORTER

(1931, 44 minutes) Film Engineering. Distributed by Fox British.

Director: Michael Powell; *Producer:* Jerome Jackson; *Screenplay:* Ralph Smart and Philip Macdonald, from a story by Philip Macdonald; *Photography:* Geoffrey Faithfull (and Michael Powell, uncredited); *Art Director:* Frank Wells

Cast: Harold French (Major Starr), Isla Bevan (Lady Susan Loman), Garry Marsh (Mendel), Spencer Trevor (Lord Longbourne), Anthony Holles (Bonzo), Noel Dainton (Colonel), Elsa Graves (Oliver), Philip Morant (Jeff)

Mendel persuades Lord Langbourne to claim the insurance money on a 'lost' diamond belonging to his daughter Lady Susan Loman, planning to steal the jewel himself. The scheme is foiled by Lady Susan's chauffeur Major Starr, actually a newspaper reporter. Mendel falls to his death following a rooftop chase and Starr marries Lady Susan.

Unpretentious and fantastic story... It is all very ingenious and is chiefly notable for the introduction of Isla Bevan, a new star, who looks like making good... Garry Marsh and Harold French both put up good performances and the picture generally is quite entertaining, if one is not too critical.
Picturegoer

HOTEL SPLENDIDE

(1932, 53 minutes) Gaumont-British. Distributed by Ideal.

Director: Michael Powell; *Producer*: Jerome Jackson; *Screenplay*: Ralph Smart, from a story by Philip Macdonald; *Photography*: Geoffrey Faithfull and Arthur Grant; *Film Editor*: John Seabourne; *Art Director*: C. Saunders; *Sound Recording*: M. Rose

Cast: Jerry Verno (Jerry Mason), Anthony Holles (Mrs Le Grange), Edgar Norfolk (Gentleman Charlie), Philip Morant (Mr Meek), Sybil Groves (Mrs Harkness), Vera Sherbourne (Joyce Dacre), Paddy Browne (Miss Meek), Michael Powell

Jerry Mason inherits a seaside hotel but is approached by a gang of crooks who have buried their loot from a robbery on the site where the hotel now stands. Mason manages to find the loot before the gang and claims the reward.

Jerry Verno is an efficient and funny comedian, and he gets away at times with this mixture of crook story and comedy which seems to fall between two stools. What laughter there is is easily accounted for but the scenes that are supposed to be thrilling miss the mark... The action takes place in a small hotel which is adequately set.
Picturegoer

* C.O.D.

(1932, 66 minutes) Westminster Films. Distributed by United Artists.

Director: Michael Powell; *Producer*: Jerome Jackson; *Screenplay*: Ralph Smart, from a story by Philip Macdonald; *Photography*: Geoffrey Faithfull; *Art Director*: Frank Wells

Cast: Garry Marsh (Peter Craven), Hope Davey (Frances), Arthur Stratton (Briggs), Sybil Grove (Mrs Briggs), Roland Culver (Edward), Peter Gawthorne (Detective), Cecil Ramage (Vyner), Bruce Belfrage (Philip)

Crime story. When Frances discovers her stepfather dead in the library, she pays Peter Craven to help hide the body. When the body turns up again, Frances is suspected of murder but Craven discovers the real criminal to be Frances' cousin Edward.

Fantastic and unconvincing crime story... Garry Marsh does his best with the rather impossible leading role, and the rest of the cast is adequate.
Picturegoer

* HIS LORDSHIP

(1932, 77 minutes) Westminster Films. Distributed by United Artists.

Director: Michael Powell; *Producer*: Jerome Jackson; *Screenplay*: Ralph Smart, based on the novel *The Right Honorable* by Oliver Madox Heuffer; *Photography*: Geoffrey Faithfull; *Music and Lyrics*: V.C. Clinton-Baddeley and Eric Maschwitz

Cast: Jerry Verno (Bert Gibbs), Janet McGrew (Ilya Myona), Ben Weldon (Washington Lincoln), Polly Ward (Leninia), Peter Gawthorne (Ferguson), Muriel George (Mrs Gibbs), Michael Hogan (Comrade Curzon), V.C. Clinton-Baddeley (Comrade Howard), Patric Ludlow (Hon Grimsthwaite)

Musical comedy. Bert Gibbs becomes a Lord but, for the sake of his mother, agrees to pose as the fiancé of movie star Ilya Myona. Bert's girl Leninia eventually wins him back.

Jerry Verno... is very badly served.. with material... which is too indefinite and poorly constructed to entertain to any extent. The story has possibilities which have not been exploited. Continuity is ragged and there is little to recommend it to discriminating patrons.
Picturegoer

* BORN LUCKY

(1932, 78 minutes) Westminster Films. Distributed by MGM (GB).

Director: Michael Powell; *Producer*: Jerome Jackson; *Screenplay*: Ralph Smart, based on the novel *Mops* by Oliver Sandys; *Art Director*: Ian Campbell-Gray

Cast: Talbot O'Farrell (Turnips), Renee Ray (Mops), John Longden (Frank Dale). Ben Welden (Harriman), Helen Ferrers (Lady Chard), Barbara Gott (Cook), Paddy Browne (Patty), Roland Gillett (John Chard)

The story of a humble girl's rise to stage fame. Mops is a waitress who becomes a successful singer and marries writer Frank Dale.

It is all very naive and the continuity is rather ragged owing to an excess of varied detail, which makes for lack of cohesion. Renee Ray as the variety artiste who becomes famous shows talent. The supporting cast is adequate. Servants' hall humour, music and songs are included.
Picturegoer

THE FIRE RAISERS

(1933, 77 minutes) Gaumont-British. Distributed by Woolf and Freedman.
Director: Michael Powell; *Producer*: Jerome Jackson; *Screenplay*: Michael Powell and Jerome
Jackson, from an original story; *Photography*: Leslie Rowson; *Film Editor*: Derek Twist; *Art
Director*: Alfred Junge; Costumes: Gordon Conway; *Sound Recording*: A.F. Birch
Cast: Leslie Banks (Jim Bronson), Anne Grey (Arden Brent), Carol Goodner (Helen Vaughan),
Frank Cellier (Brent), Francis L Sullivan (Stedding), Laurence Anderson (Twist), Harry Caine
(Bates), Joyce Kirby (Polly), George Merritt (Sonners)

Fire assessor Jim Bronson uses unscrupulous tactics to build his own business. When
he loses it all at the gambling table he joins a group of arsonists but later helps the
police to round them up.

*Though this film is by no means a continuous blaze, its fires are certainly worth seeing... Francis
Sullivan plays the part of the chief villain with real imagination... The road to ruin is described
with some plausibility and not without some entertainment on the way, including a few excellent
scenes of horse-racing.*
The Times

*We have shouted so long and so loudly for a journalistic talkie... that it may seem a bit ingra-
cious to grumble when we get it. Gaumont-British deserve full credit for putting the topical theme
of incendiarism on the screen, and for getting the fim out while the subject is still front page
news. Their mistake is in making it so obviously a stop-press item.*
The Observer

THE NIGHT OF THE PARTY

(US: The Murder Party)
(1934, 61 minutes) Gaumont-British.
Director: Michael Powell; *Producer*: Jerome Jackson; *Screenplay*: Ralph Smart, based on the stage
play by Roland Pertwee and John Hastings Turner; *Photography*: Glen MacWilliams; *Art Director*:
Alfred Junge; *Costumes*: Gordon Conway; *Sound Recording*: S. Jolly
Cast: Leslie Banks (Sir John Holland), Ian Hunter (Guy Kennington), Jane Baxter (Peggy
Studholme), Ernest Thesiger (Chiddiatt), Viola Keats (John Holland), Malcolm Keen (Lord
Studholme), Jane Millican (Anna Chiddiatt), Muriel Akad (Princess), John Turnbull (Ramage),
Laurence Anderson (Defence Counsel), W. Graham Brown (General Piddington)

Murder mystery. Ruthless newspaper owner Lord Studholme gives a dinner party in
honour of a foreign princess. When a party game of murder organized by Studholme
ends with the host actually murdered, it seems that each guest has a motive for wanti-
ng him dead.

*Lacking in ingenuity and wildly incredible in the denouement, the mystery is very slowly devel-
oped, and the acting fair.*
Picturegoer

RED ENSIGN

(US: Strike!)
(1934, 69 minutes) Gaumont-British.
Director: Michael Powell; *Producer:* Jerome Jackson; *Screenplay*: Michael Powell and Jerome
Jackson; *Additional Dialogue*: L. du Garde Peach; *Director of Photography*: Leslie Rowson; *Art
Director*: Alfred Junge; *Costumes*: Gordon Conway; *Sound Recording*: G. Birch

Cast: Leslie Banks (David Barr), Carol Goodner (June MacKinnon), Frank Vosper (Lord Dean), Alfred Drayton (Manning), Donald Calthrop (MacLeod), Allan Jeayes (Emerson), Campbell Gullan (Hannay), Percy Parsons (Casey), Fewlass Llewellyn (Sir Gregory), Henry Oscar (Raglan), John Laurie

David Barr is a ship builder aiming to launch a new type of vessel. When the board of directors back out of financing the project, Barr puts forward his own money but is later caught forging his chairman's signature on a cheque and is sent to gaol. On his release, the ship is finally launched and he is reunited with his fiancée June who stood by him.

I applaud this film because it is an attempt to put an important part of Britain on the map… Michael Powell, the director, handles his crowds well. His cutting and camera angles are good, but he should beware of treating a subject in the abstract so that it is like a chess problem.
Sunday Express

The story of British shipbuilding has been going begging for a long time as the subject of an epic British film. It is still going begging. Gaumont-British have had the wisdom to snap it up but not the wisdom to realise that it should have been their big picture of the year. Jerry Jackson and Michael Powell have used the shipyards as the background to an excellent, high-speed melodrama; the story is eventful, the acting brisk and the treatment popular, but there is nothing epic about the production.
The Observer

SOMETHING ALWAYS HAPPENS

(1934, 69 minutes) Warner Brothers-First National.
Director: Michael Powell; *Executive Producer*: Irving Asher; *Screenplay*: Brock Williams; *Photography*: Basil Emmott; *Art Director*: Peter Proud; *Film Editor*: Ralph Dawson; *Costumes*: Louis Brooks; *Sound Recording*: Leslie Murray, H.C. Pearson
Cast: Ian Hunter (Peter Middleton), Nancy O'Neil (Cynthia Hatch), John Singer (Billy), Peter Gawthorne (Mr Hatch), Muriel George (Mrs Badger), Barry Livesey (George Hamlin), Millicent Wolf (Glenda), Louie Emery (Mrs Tremlett), Reg Marcus (Coster), George Zucco (Café Proprietor)

Unemployed car salesman Peter Middleton is encouraged by his girlfriend Cynthia to approach the head of a car factory with his suggestion for making petrol stations more attractive to customers. When the owner rejects the idea, Peter joins a rival company and becomes a great success. He is eventually taken home by Cynthia to meet her father – the first company's manager – who realizes his mistake and gives the pair his blessing.

Neatly constructed and excellently dialogued comedy… Ian Hunter gives a very good perfor-mance… Michael Powell's direction is apt and imaginative, and the comedy situations are han-dled with a slickness that makes this unpretentious picture a very enjoyable one.
Picturegoer

* THE GIRL IN THE CROWD

(1934, 52 minutes) First National.
Director: Michael Powell; *Executive Producer*: Irving Asher; *Screenplay*: Brock Williams; *Photography*: Basil Emmott; *Film Editor*: Bert Bates
Cast: Barry Clifton (David Gordon), Patricia Hilliard (Marian), Googie Withers (Sally), Harold

● Seventeen-year-old Googie Withers (left) makes her screen debut in *The Girl in the Crowd*, a 'lost' quota picture directed by Michael Powell in 1934. Just four years later she went up for a leading role in *The Lady Vanishes*. 'Funnily enough, in those days if you were playing a leading part – even in quickies – you somehow thought that you should be playing leads for Mr Hitchcock. I took it rather badly when I was offered a small part!'

French (Bob), Clarence Blakiston (Mr Peabody), Margaret Gunn (Joyce), Richard Littledale (Bill Manners), Phyllis Morris (Mrs Lewis), Patric Knowles (Tom Burrows), Marjorie Corbett (Secretary), Brenda Lawless (Policewoman), Barbara Waring (Mannequin), Eve Lister (Ruby), Betty Lyne (Phyllis), Melita Bell (Assistant Manageress), John Wood (Harry)

Bookseller David Gordon's new wife Marian has never met David's friend Bob but by telephone advises him on how to attract women by following the first attractive girl he sees. Unfortunately, the girl turns out to be Marian and Bob is arrested for insulting behaviour and taken to court, but his police friends manage to sort things out for him.

Some well devised situations, and sound technical polish help to brighten up the otherwise flimsy and disjointed plot of this mildly amusing comedy. It is a trifling affair, weak in continuity but generally competently directed, although occasionally there is an atmosphere of amateur theatricals about it.
Picturegoer

LAZYBONES

(1935, 65 minutes) A Real Art Film. Distributed by Radio Pictures.
Director: Michael Powell; *Producer:* Julius Hagen; *Screenplay:* Gerald Fairlie, adapted from a play by Ernest Denny; *Photography:* Ernest Palmer; *Film Editor:* Ralph Kemplen; *Art Direction:* James A. Carter; *Sound Recording:* Leo Wilkins; *Assistant Director:* Fred V. Merrick; *Coiffure:* Charles
Cast: Ian Hunter (Sir Reginald Ford), Claire Luce (Kitty McCarthy), Bernard Nedell (Michael McCarthy), Denys Blakelock (Hugh Ford), Mary Gaskell (Marjory Ford), Michael Shepley

(Hildebrand Pope), Pamela Carme (Lottie Pope), Bobbie Comber (Kemp), Fred Withers (Richards), Sarah Allgood (Bridget), Frank Morgan (Tom), Fewlass Llewellyn (Lord Brockley), Harold Warrender (Lord Melton), Paul Blake (Viscount Woodland), Miles Malleson (Pessimist)

Reginald Ford – the 'lazybones' of the title – is encouraged by his penniless father to marry American heiress, Kitty McCarthy who turns out also to be penniless after being swindled by her advisers. Reginald recovers documents stolen by Kitty's brother Mike who planned to use them to raise money. Sending Mike back to America, Reginald marries Kitty anyway.

Simple comedy, quite well presented and competently acted. Ian Hunter makes his artificial role attractive by the strength of his personality, and Claire Luce is quite glamorous as the wife.
Picturegoer

THE LOVE TEST

(1935, 63 minutes) Fox British.
Director: Michael Powell; *Producer*: Leslie L. Landau; *Screenplay*: Selwyn Jepson, based on a story by Jack Celestin; *Photography*: Arthur Crabtree
Cast: Judy Gunn (Mary Lee), Louis Hayward (John Gregg), Googie Withers (Minnie), Dave Hutcheson (Thompson), Morris Harvey (President), Aubrey Dexter (Vice President), Jack Knight (Managing Director), Gilbert Davis (Smith, Chief Chemist), Eve Turner (Kathleen), Bernard Miles (Allan), Shayle Gardner (Night Watchman), James Craig (Boilerman), Thorley Walters, Ian Wilson

Mary Lee is appointed head of a laboratory looking for a process to fireproof celluloid. Resentful of her position, Thompson and his male colleagues plan to make her fall in love with John so that she will neglect her work, but the couple really do fall in love. Thompson tricks Mary into firing John just as he has discovered the formula, and

● **Pretty heroine Judy Gunn with Louis Hayward in** *The Love Test*, **an interesting romantic drama made by Powell in 1935.**

attempts to claim the work as his own, but Mary realizes what has happened and John is reinstated.

The idea of the film is better than its carrying out. The setting is unusual and interesting... it is quite good light entertainment for the average filmgoer. Adequate as a piece of screen work.
Monthly Film Bulletin

THE PHANTOM LIGHT

(1935, 76 minutes) Gainsborough. Presented by Gaumont-British.
Director: Michael Powell; *Producer*: Jerome Jackson; *Screenplay*: Ralph Smart, based on the play *The Haunted Light* by Evadne Price and Joan Roy Byford; *Additional Dialogue*: J. Jefferson Farjeon and Austin Melford; *Photography*: Roy Kellino; *Film Editor*: Derek Twist; *Art Director*: Alex Vetchinsky; *Music Score*: Louis Levy; *Sound Recordist*: A. Birch
Cast: Binnie Hale (Alice Bright), Gordon Harker (Sam Higgins), Donald Calthrop (David Owen), Milton Rosmer (Dr Carey), Ian Hunter (Jim Pearce), Herbert Lomas (Claff Owen), Reginald Tate (Tom Evans), Barry O'Neill (Captain Pearce), Mickey Brantford (Bob Peters), Alice O'Day (Mrs Owen), Fewlass Llewellyn (Griffith Owen), Edgar K. Bruce (Sergeant Owen), Louie Emery (Station Mistress)

New keeper Sam Higgins is sent to North Stack lighthouse where ships have been lost on the nearby rocks. Jim Pearce deliberately maroons himself on the rock along with Alice Bright. When the light is later smashed, Jim reveals that his brother's ship is the wreckers' latest target, while Alice is a detective sent to investigate. Jim alerts the coastguard as Sam and Alice relight the beacon and avert a tragedy. Trapped on the lighthouse, saboteur Dr Carey leaps to his death rather than face capture.

Milton Rosmer... and Herbert Lomas... are outstanding among an able supporting cast. There are some delightful shots of the harbour, gulls and fishing trawlers, and sea beating into rocky inlets. I cannot imagine why the appeal of this most attractive scenery has not commended itself to other British directors other than Michael Powell, whose treatment of this film as a whole is excellent.
Sunday Times

A very strong melodrama, atmospheric to a marked degree.
Variety

A melodramatic thriller with plenty of fun in it... Gordon Harker is excellently cast... The atmosphere is well built up and sustained, and the tension is balanced by the comic relief. The photography is very good, giving some fine views of Welsh landscape and of the village where the drama takes place... There are a number of violent scenes which make the film unsuitable for young people or impressionable adolescents.
Monthly Film Bulletin

* THE PRICE OF A SONG

(1935, 67 minutes) Fox British.
Producer and Director: Michael Powell; *Scenarist*: Michael Barringer, from an original story by Anthony Gittens; *Photography:* Jimmy Wilson
Cast: Campbell Gullan (Arnold Grierson), Marjorie Corbett (Margaret Nevern), Gerald Fielding (Michael Hardwicke), Dora Barton (Letty Grierson), Charles Mortimer (Oliver Broom), Oriel Ross (Elsie), Henry Caine (Stringer), Sybil Grove (Mrs Bancroft), Eric Maturin (Nevern), Felix Aylmer (Graham), Cynthia Stock (Mrs Bush), Mavis Clair (Maudie Bancroft)

Refused a loan by his songwriter son-in-law Nevern, Arnold Grierson murders

Nervern as he is playing his latest composition. Michael Hardwick discovers the body and is accused of the murder. At the reading of the will, Grierson is revealed as the murderer when he whistles Nevern's new, unpublished composition which he could only have heard on the night of the murder.

* SOMEDAY

(1935, 68 minutes) Warner Brothers-First National.

Director: Michael Powell; *Producer*: Irving Asher; *Screenplay*: Brock Williams, based on the novel *Young Nowheres* by I. A. R. Wylie; *Photography*: Basil Emmott; *Film Editor*: Bert Bates; *Art Director*: Ian Campbell-Gray

Cast: Margaret Lockwood (Emily); Esmond Knight (Curley Blake), Henry Mollison (Canley), Sunday Wilshin (Betty), Raymond Lovell (Carr), Ivor Bernard (Hope), George Pughe (Milkman), Jane Cornell (Nurse)

Lift operator Curley is in love with Emily, a cleaner working in the same block. When Emily is released from hospital, Curley arranges a surprise dinner for her in the flat of Mr Carr who is away. When Carr returns unexpectedly, a fight breaks out, with Curley being charged with illegal entry and assault. They are rescued by Curley's play-boy employer, Canley.

This is a pleasant unpretentious story pleasantly told. The direction, however, lacks polish and is not convincing...While the photography is uninteresting, it is exceptionally clear and well done. Esmond Knight does not appear too happy as 'Curley' but Margaret Lockwood is quite successful as Emily.
Monthly Film Bulletin

HER LAST AFFAIRE

(1936, 78 minutes) New Ideal.

Director: Michael Powell; *Producer*: Simon Rowson and Geoffrey Rowsn; *Screenplay*: Ian Dalrymple, based on the play S.O.S. by Walter Ellis; *Photography*: Leslie Rowson; *Film Editor*: Ian Dalrymple; *Art Director*: J. Elder Wills; *Sound Recording*: George Burgess; *Assistant Director*: Sidney Stone

Cast: Hugh Williams (Alan Heriot), Viola Keats (Lady Avril Weyre), Francis L. Sullivan (Sir Julian Weyre), Sophie Stewart (Judy Weyre), Googie Withers (Effie), Felix Aylmer (Lord Carnforth), Cecil Parker (Sir Arthur Harding), John Gardner (Boxall), Henry Caine (Inspector Marsh), Gerrard Tyrell (Martin), John Laurie (Innkeeper)

Lady Avril Weyre, the wife of a promising politician, is found dead at a country inn where she had been accompanied by her husband's secretary, Alan Heriot. Heriot is immediately under suspicion, although he had taken her there solely to gain informa-tion which would exonerate his father. He is eventually cleared, and marries Lady Avril's daughter Judy.

The story is not redeemed by any outstanding performances by the actors and the attempts to reveal the characters' thoughts by flashes-back are confusing rather than helpful.
Monthly Film Bulletin

* THE BROWN WALLET

(1936, 68 minutes) Warner Brothers-First National.

Director: Michael Powell; *Producer*: Irving Asher; *Screenplay*: Ian Dalrymple, from a story by Stacy Aumonier; *Photography*: Basil Emmott

Cast: Patric Knowles (John Gillespie), Nancy O'Neill (Eleanor), Henry Caine (Simmonds), Henrietta Watson (Aunt Mary), Charlotte Leigh (Miss Barton), Shayle Gardner (Wotherspoone), Edward Dalby (Minting), Eliot Makeham (Hobday), Bruce Winston (Julian Thorpe), Jane Millican (Miss Bloxham), Louis Goodrich (Coroner), Dick Francis, George Mills (Detectives)

Penniless John Gillespie is refused a loan by wealthy Aunt Mary, but on the way home finds a wallet containing £2,000 which he keeps. Visited later by police investigating the suspicious death of his aunt he is placed under suspicion of murder until it is discovered that her butler is the real killer. Left a considerable sum in his aunt's will, John returns the original £2,000 to its owner.

The cast works hard to portray the series of types which they are called on to represent, but there is a lack of directiveness about the production which prevents the development of the tension which should be an integral part of a 'murder' film.
Monthly Film Bulletin

CROWN V STEVENS

(1936, 66 minutes) Warner Brothers-First National.
Director: Michael Powell; *Producer*: Irving Asher; *Screenplay*: Brock Williams, based on the novel *Third Time Unlucky* by Laurence Maynell; *Photography*: Basil Emmott; *Film Editor*: Bert Bates; *Art Director*: Peter Proud; *Sound Recording*: Leslie Murray, H.C. Pearson
Cast: Beatrix Thomson (Doris Stevens), Patric Knowles (Chris Jansen), Reginald Purdell (Alf), Glennis Lorimer (Molly), Allan Jeayes (Inspector Carter), Frederick Piper (Arthur Stevens), Googie Withers (Ella), Mabel Poulton (Mamie), Morris Harvey (Julius Bayleck), Billy Watts (Joe Andrews), Davina Craig (Maggie), Bernard Miles (Detective)

Doris Stevens commits a murder and then tries to poison her husband, involving his employee Jansen who was a witness to the earlier crime. Jansen saves Stevens and persuades Doris to give herself up to the police.

Conventional murder mystery drama adequately produced and acted. Average quota thriller. No use to children.
Kine Weekly

* THE MAN BEHIND THE MASK

(1936, 79 minutes) Joe Rock Studios. Distributed by MGM (GB).
Director: Michael Powell; *Producer*: Joe Rock; *Screenplay*: Ian Hay, Sidney Courtenay, Stanley Hayes; *Scenario:* Jack Byrd from the novel *The Chase of the Golden Plate* by Jacques Futrelle; *Photography*: Ernest Palmer
Cast: Hugh Williams (Nick Barclay), Jane Baxter (June Slade), Maurice Schwartz (The Master), Donald Calthrop (Dr Walpole), Henry Oscar (Officer), Peter Gawthorne (Lord Slade), Kitty Kelly (Miss Weeks), Ronald Ward (Jimmy Slade), George Merritt (Mallory), Reginald Tate (Hayden), Ivor Bernard (Hewitt), Hal Gordon (Sergeant), Gerald Fielding (Harah), Barbara Everest (Lady Slade), Wilf Caithness (Butler), Moyra Fagan (Nora), Sid Crossley (Postman)

Nick Barclay and June Slade plan to elope from a masked ball when Nick is attacked by a man who takes his mask and kidnaps June, also stealing the Shield of Kahm, which June's father Lord Slade has just acquired. Nick manages to rescue June and the Shield, but then both are tricked, along with Lord Slade, into going to a house where the leader of an international gang intends to retake the Shield. The police arrive and the crooks are arrested.

The story is melodramatic and absurd, but technically the film is excellent. Direction, photography, lighting, acting and sound are all good... All the acting is competent but Donald Calthrop... and Kitty Kelley... give the most polished performances. On the whole, the director is to be most congratulated for having made what must be termed a good film out of very unlikely material.
Monthly Film Bulletin

THE EDGE OF THE WORLD

(1937, 81 minutes) Rock Studios.

Director: Michael Powell; *Producer:* Joe Rock; *Original Story and Screenplay:* Michael Powell; *Photography:* Ernest Palmer, Skeets Kelly and Monty Berman; *Film Editor:* Derek Twist; *Assistant Editor:* Bob Walters; *Music Score*: Cyril Ray; *Orchestrations*: W.L. Williamson; *Chorus*: Women of the Glasgow Orpheus Choir; *Sound Supervisor*: L.K. Tregellas; *Sound Recording*: W.H.O. Sweeney; *Production Staff*: Gerard Blattner, John Seabourne, Vernon C. Sewell, W.H. Farr, George Black, Sydney Streeter

Cast: John Laurie (Peter Manson), Belle Chrystall (Ruth Manson), Finlay Currie (James Gray), Niall MacGinnis (Andrew Gray), Eric Berry (Robbie Manson), Kitty Kirwan (Jean Manson), Grant Sutherland (The Catechist), Campbell Robson (The Laird), George Summers (Skipper), Margaret Grieg (Baby). With: Michael Powell (Graham), Frankie Reidy (Mrs Graham) and the people of the island of Foula

Harsh winters and poor harvests have left the crofters of remote Scottish island Hirta with a failing supply of food and peat for warmth. Families are bitterly divided: Robbie Manson and James Gray insist that the island folk should leave for the mainland, but neither Gray's son Andrew nor Robbie's father Peter want to leave their homes. Andrew and Robbie aim to settle the argument in the traditional manner by a race up the cliffs but Robbie falls and is killed. Holding Andrew responsible, Peter refuses to allow him to marry his daughter Ruth and the young man despondently leaves the island to find work on the mainland.

Months later, Andrew learns that Ruth has given birth to his child who is seriously ill but cut off from the mainland by the treacherous seas. As he returns to take the child to safety, the islanders reluctantly accept that the rock will no longer sustain their old way of life and prepare to be evacuated. As the boats are loaded, Peter makes one last climb of the cliffs, but falls to his death. The people of Hirta leave their crofts for the last time and sail for the mainland as Andrew raises a monument to Peter, who ultimately did not leave his island home.

It is impossible to overpraise the grandeur of the natural settings of The Edge of the World. *The cliffs are awe-inspiring in their bleakness; the reality of their danger is very obvious in the finely staged scenes of the climbing contest... Rich character study also is there; few more impressive scenes have been filmed than the Elder's round of the island.*
Motion Picture Herald

The normal life on the island in its simplicity and with its hardships is portrayed effectively by the islanders themselves. The professional actors have a difficult task to render credible the incidents which make up the story... it remains Foula which is both hero and heroine of this film, and its appeal will be to lovers of magnificent scenes of natural beauty.
Monthly Film Bulletin

Unfortunately, most skilled documentalists are not experienced in dealing with human material... That fact reveals the unique ability of Michael Powell... Throughout his film there are touches revealing his understanding of reality in relation to the screen... Powell never forgets the wild

Filmography

beauty around him...With The Edge of the World *the Fictional-Documentary film has arrived.*
Andrew Buchanan, Sight and Sound

WHAT MEN LIVE BY

(1939, 42 minutes)
Director: Vernon Sewell. *Screenplay:* Vernon Sewell (and Michael Powell, uncredited) from the story by Tolstoy; *Photography:* George Pocknall; *Assistant Director:* William Farr
Cast: includes Esmond Knight

THE SPY IN BLACK

(US: U-Boat 29)
(1939, 82 minutes) Harefield Films.
Director: Michael Powell; *Producer:* Irving Asher; *Screenplay:* Emeric Pressburger, from the novel by J. Storer Clouston; *Scenario:* Rodney Ackland; *Director of Photography:* Bernard Browne; *Supervising Film Editor:* William Hornbeck; *Film Editor:* Hugh Stewart; *Assistant Editor:* John Guthrie; *Production Design:* Vincent Korda; *Art Director:* Frederick Pusey; *Music Score:* Miklos Rozsa; *Music Director:* Muir Mathieson; *Sound Recording:* A.W. Watkins
Cast: Conrad Veidt (Captain Hardt), Sebastian Shaw (Lt Ashington), Valerie Hobson (Schoolmistress), Marius Goring (Lt Schuster), Hay Petrie (Engineer), Cyril Raymond (Rev John Harris), Athole Stewart (Rev Hector Matthews), Agnes Laughlan (Mrs Matthews), Helen Haye (Mrs Sedley), Mary Morris (Chauffeur), June Duprez (Anne Burnett), Torin Thatcher (Submarine Officer), Grant Sutherland (Bob Bratt), Margaret Moffatt (Kate), Robert Rendel (Admiral), George Summers (Captain Ratter), Kenneth Warrington (Commander Denis), Bernard Miles (Hotel Desk Clerk), Esma Cannon, Kenneth Warrington, Skelton Knaggs

German submarine commander Captain Hardt lands at Malkirk, one of the Orkney Islands on the northern coast of Scotland, where his contact, the schoolmistress, tells him that he is to sink ten British ships in the local harbour with the help of a treacherous British seaman, Lieutenant Ashington. Unknown to Hardt, both Ashington and the girl are working for British intelligence, who have intercepted the real German spy and replaced her with a British agent.

Ashington arranges for the girl to leave on a ferry carrying prisoners-of-war, but Hardt escapes on the same vessel and leads a group of Germans to mutiny and take over the ship, only for it to be torpedoed by his own submarine. A British destroyer lifts the passengers off the stricken ferry, but Hardt refuses the offer of help. His submarine, meanwhile, has been sunk by the British fleet, its crew perishing in the same waters as their captain.

This intricate story is gripping from beginning to end, and very skillfully (sic) directed. It has abundance of thrilling incidents, effective suspense values and spectacular sea scenes. The climax is grim but logical... Conrad Veidt is brilliant in the lead. He is throughout a tragic if slightly sinister figure, and wins respect and sympathy as a patriot with the qualities most admirable and admired in soldier, sailor or airman of any nationality – loyalty, courage, obedience and steadfast endurance... The remaining players are all excellent in their different ways... The atmosphere is realistic and convincing, the photography noteworthy. Pictures of Scapa Flow, of the Orkney Islands, and of the Fleet are particularly effective.
Monthly Film Bulletin

...a praiseworthy film on international espionage during World War One... The plot, while

necessarily melodramatic, is always within the range of possibility... Conrad Veidt... has a strong role for which he's admirably suited. Sebastian Shaw is excellent as the English naval officer. Valerie Hobson, as the other spy, is creditable.
Variety

THE LION HAS WINGS

(1939, 76 minutes) London Films.
Director: Michael Powell, Brian Desmond Hurst and Adrian Brunel; *Producer:* Alexander Korda; *Screenplay:* Adrian Brunel and E.V.H. Emmett, from an original story by Ian Dalrymple; *Director of Photography:* Harry Stradling; *Additional Photography:* Osmond Borrowdale; *Camera Operator:* Bernard Browne; *Art Director:* Vincent Korda; *Supervising Film Editor:* William Hornbeck; *Film Editors:* Henry Cornelius and Charles Frend; *Music Score:* Richard Addinsell; *Music Director:* Muir Mathieson; *Sound Recording:* A.W. Watkins; *Associate Producer:* Ian Dalrymple; *Technical Adviser:* Squadron Leader H.M.S. Wright
Cast: Ralph Richardson (Wing Commander Richardson), Merle Oberon (Mrs Richardson), June Duprez (June), Derrick de Marney (Bill), Austin Trevor (Schulemburg), Robert Douglas (Briefing Officer), Anthony Bushell (Pilot), Herbert Lomas (Holveg), Brian Worth (Bobby), Ivan Brandt (Officer), Milton Rosmer (Head of Observer Corps), Robert Rendel (Chief of Staff), G.H. Mulcaster (Controller), Archibald Batty (Air Officer), Bernard Miles, Miles Malleson, Charles Carson, John Penrose, Ronald Adam, John Longden, Ian Fleming, Frank Tickle, John Robinson, Carl Jaffe, Gerald Case, Torin Thatcher, Ronald Shiner, E.V.H. Emmett (Narrator – GB version), Lowell Thomas (Narrator – US version)

A semi-documentary, opening with scenes of everyday life in 1937 Britain and focusing on families who have connections with the Royal Air Force, in particular Wing Commander Richardson, his wife and their young Canadian cousin Bobby who is engaged to Merle's friend June. As the Nazi rise in Germany spreads across Europe, so in 1939 war is declared. The RAF is shown ready to defend the nation, raiding Kiel before the film closes with a demonstration of Britain's defences against air attack.

This picture, sponsored by the Ministry of Information and produced in six weeks by Alexander Korda, can best be described as a tour de force... [it] is a supreme example of what can be done by skilled cutting and direction. Even more, it admirably fulfils its object – to inspire quiet confidence in the hearts of those who see it.
Monthly Film Bulletin

CONTRABAND

(US: Blackout)
(1940, 92 minutes, US: 80 minutes) British National Pictures.
Director: Michael Powell; *Producer:* John Corfield; *Original Story and Screenplay:* Emeric Pressburger; *Scenario:* Michael Powell and Brock Williams; *Director of Photography:* F.A. Young; *Art Director:* Alfred Junge; *Film Editor:* John Seabourne; *Music Score:* Richard Addinsell and John Greenwood; *Music Director:* Muir Mathieson; *White Negro cabaret designed and executed by* Hedley Briggs; *Sound Recording:* A.W. Watkins and C.C. Stevens; *Associate Producer:* Roland Gillett; *Production Manager:* Anthony Nelson Keys
Cast: Conrad Veidt (Captain Andersen), Valerie Hobson (Mrs Sorensen/'Miss Clayton'), Hay Petrie (Skold, Mate of SS *Helvig*/Chef of *Three Vikings*), Joss Ambler (Lt Cmdr Ashton), Raymond Lovell (Van Dyne), Esmond Knight (Mr Pidgeon), Charles Victor (Hendrick), Phoebe Kershaw (Miss Lang), Harold Warrender (Lt Cmdr Ellis), Eric Maturin, John Longden (Passport Officers), Paddy Browne (Singer), Henry Wolston, Julian Vedey, Sydney Moncton, Hamilton Keen (Danish Waiters), Leo Genn, Peter Bull, Stuart Lathan (The Brothers Grimm), Dennis Arundell (Lieman),

Eric Berry (Mr Abo), Olga Edwards (Mrs Abo), Molly Hamley Clifford (Baroness Hekla), Tony Gable (Mrs Karoly), Desmond Jeans, Eric Hales (Karolys), Jean Roberts (Hanson), Manning Whiley (Manager of Mousetrap), Bernard Miles (Belligerent pipe smoker), Esma Cannon (Danish waitress), Torin Thatcher (Port Officer)

Neutral Danish steamship *Helvig*, returning from America, runs foul of British contraband regulations and is led to a control port where Captain Andersen grudgingly allows inspection by British officers with the promise that the ship will be allowed to proceed in the morning. Discovering that his landing passes have been stolen and two passengers are missing – Mrs Sorensen and Mr Pidgeon, both agents for British Naval Intelligence – Andersen rows ashore, following the two escapees on to a train bound for London.

Pidgeon escapes in the London black-out but Andersen catches up with Mrs Sorensen. Both are captured by German Intelligence, who substitute false plans for those carried by Mrs Sorensen. Andersen escapes and recruits help from a Danish restaurant nearby. They rescue Mrs Sorensen who then slips away to inform the Admiralty of the true message which she is carrying. Passengers and crew return to the *Helvig* in time to sail as arranged the next morning, when Andersen learns that Naval Intelligence had been monitoring the events of the previous evening and he is congratulated on his night's work.

About the best British thriller I've seen. Much of it is a great deal more than thriller. There's a vivid and I imagine accurate picture of the British contraband control people at work... Then there's a chase through the black-out in London, the atmosphere of which I can vouch for as entirely authentic.
The Listener

This exciting story is dramatically put over and excellently directed. The comparison between the British and German methods of dealing with neutrals is not too heavily stressed and is all the more convincing as a result. Conrad Veidt, as the resourceful, courageous captain gives a brilliant performance while Valerie Hobson not only looks charming but acts extremely well... Hay Petrie provides some excellent comic relief.
Monthly Film Bulletin

THE THIEF OF BAGDAD

(1940, 106 minutes) Technicolor. London Films.

Directors: Ludwig Berger, Michael Powell and Tim Whelan (and Zoltan Korda, William Cameron Menzies and Alexander Korda, uncredited); *Producer*: Alexander Korda; *Associate Producer*: Zoltan Korda; *Screenplay*: Lajos Biro; *Dialogue*: Miles Malleson; *Director of Photography*: Georges Périnal; *Camera Operator*: Robert Krasker; *Additional Photography*: Osmond Borrodale; *Special Effects*: Lawrence Butler; *Film Editor*: Charles Crichton; *Art Direction*: Vincent Korda; *Associate Art Directors*: W. Percy Day, William Cameron Menzies, Frederick Pusey, Ferdinand Bellan; *Music Score*: Miklos Rozsa; *Costumes*: Oliver Messel, John Armstrong, Marcel Vertes; *Sound Recording*: A.W. Watkins

Cast: Conrad Veidt (Jaffar), Sabu (Abu), June

● **Conrad Veidt as evil vizier Jaffar in Korda's *Thief of Bagdad*.**

Duprez (Princess), John Justin (Ahmad), Rex Ingram (Djinni), Miles Malleson (Sultan), Mary Morris (Halima), Hay Petrie (Astrologer), Morton Selten (King), Roy Emmerton (Jailer), Allan Jeayes (Storyteller), Adelaide Hall (Singer), Glynis Johns, Norman Pierce, Otto Wallen, Henry Hallett, John Salew

Imprisoned by Grand Vizier Jaffar, Ahmad, rightful King of Bagdad, escapes with Abu to Bastra, where Ahmad falls in love with the Princess. Her father, the Sultan offers his daughter to Jaffar in return for a flying horse. When Abu releases the giant Djinni from a bottle, he is granted three wishes. Abu secures the All-Seeing Eye from the highest Temple in the World, with which he and Ahmad view Jaffar about to marry the Princess.

The Djinni inadvertently returns Ahmad to the palace, where he and the Princess are captured by Jaffar. Abu, meanwhile, encounters the Old King who gives him a magic carpet on which he flies back to Bagdad. Jaffar has killed the Sultan and attempts to escape on the flying horse but is killed by Abu's magic arrow. Ahmad and his Princess are united at last, but Abu sets off on his flying carpet for further adventures.

In this most lavish production the carefully planned colour scheme and the skilful use of the camera make the film one of the most satisfactory colour films yet created. Sabu makes an excellent thief and goes through his adventures with an almost Cockney nimbleness of wit and hand. June Duprez and John Justin make a pair of handsome lovers and Conrad Veidt is the wickedest of Grand Viziers... Extensive use is made of trick photography and this is the least satisfactory aspect of the production.
Monthly Film Bulletin

The wonder is that with so many years and directors and co-directors gone to its making, it is so good.
New Statesman

49th PARALLEL
(US: The Invaders)
(1941, 123 minutes, US: 104 minutes) Ortus films / Ministry of Information.
Producer and Director: Michael Powell; *Original Story and Screenplay*: Emeric Pressburger; *Scenario*: Rodney Ackland, Emeric Pressburger; *Director of Photography*: Frederick Young; *Camera Operators*: Skeets Kelly, Henty Henty-Creer; *Film Editor*: David Lean; *Associate Editor*: Hugh Stewart; *Backgrounds*: Osmond Borrowdale; *Art Director*: David Rawnsley; *Associate Art Director*: Sydney Streeter, Frederick Pusey; *Music Score*: Ralph Vaughan Williams; *Music Director*: Muir Mathieson; *Sound Supervisor*: A.W. Watkins; *Sound Recording*: C.C. Stevens, Walter Darling; *Associate Producer*: Roland Gillett, George Brown; *Production Supervisor*: Harold Boxall; *Assistant Director*: Alan Seabourne; *Canadian Adviser*: Nugent M. Clougher
Cast: Leslie Howard (Philip Armstrong Scott), Laurence Olivier (Johnnie, the Trapper), Raymond Massey (Andy Brock), Anton Walbrook (Peter), Eric Portman (Lieutenant Hirth), Richard George (Kommandant Bernsdorff), Raymond Lovell (Lieutenant Kuhnecker), Niall MacGinnis (Vogel), Peter Moore (Krantz), John Chandos (Lohrmann), Basil Appleby (Jahner), Finlay Currie (Factor), Ley On (Nick, the Eskimo), Glynis Johns (Anna), Charles Victor (Andreas), Frederick Piper (David), Tawera Moana (George the Indian), Eric Clavering (Art), Charles Rolfe (Bob), Theodore Salt, O.W. Fonger (US Customs Officers), Vincent Massey (Narrator)

A German submarine is destroyed in Hudson Bay, leaving a five-man shore party, led by Lieutenant Kuhnecker, stranded on Canadian soil. Reaching a trading post, they overpower the Factor and Canadian trapper Johnnie Barras, who attempts to shout a warning over the short wave radio and is shot. A plane sent to investigate is hijacked by the Germans, but crashes into a lake, killing Kuhnecker. Lieutenant Hirth takes command, leading the four survivors to a Hutterite camp of German refugees led by Peter. Hirth asks his 'fellow Germans' for their help in spreading the movement across Canada, but Peter denounces him as a fanatic. When Vogel chooses to remain with the community, he is executed by his comrades as a deserter.

At Vancouver Kranz is arrested by the Mounted Police while Hirth and Lohrmann escape to the Rockies. There they encounter Englishman Philip Armstrong Scott, researching Indian folklore. Taken captive, Scott manages to break free and capture Lohrmann. Alone, Hirth boards a freight train headed for the neutral United States. Also in the car is Canadian soldier Andy Brock. At the border, Hirth surrenders to customs officers and asks to be taken to the German embassy, but Brock persuades them to wheel the carriage back into Canada where he can show the German what he thinks of the Nazi order.

49th Parallel *is an adventure story, and a bit more. The bit more interests me, because it makes and mars. The difficulty is that the natural heroes of its adventure are the campaigning Nazis. The further they get... the more inclined shall we be to sympathise. However, if the case for Democracy, a thrilling adventure, a constellation of actors and a landscape album can be crammed into one film, here it is.*
New Statesman, *18 October 1941*

An important and effective propaganda film... the strongest possible indictment against Nazism. Script, by Emeric Pressburger, is direct and forceful. Michael Powell... has managed to maintain his stature among the top directors.
Variety

Michael Powell is to be congratulated on his persistence with this at first apparently ill-starred film. It is an admirable piece of work from every point of view and credit should be given to everyone connected with the finished product... The acting throughout is admirable; even so there is a temptation to say the honours go to Eric Portman as the leader of the Nazis. His performance right through the film puts him in the star class of film actors.
Monthly Film Bulletin, *October 1941*

AN AIRMAN'S LETTER TO HIS MOTHER

(1941, 5 minutes) Distributed by MGM.
Produced, Directed and Photographed: Michael Powell; *Additional Photography*: Bernard Browne

Narrated by John Gielgud, the letter in question had appeared in *The Times*, written by a pilot who had since been killed in the war. Powell personally produced and photographed the film with assistance from Bernard Browne.

ONE OF OUR AIRCRAFT IS MISSING

(1942, 102 minutes, US: 82 minutes) The Archers/British National.
Written, Produced and Directed for The Archers: Michael Powell and Emeric Pressburger;
Original Story: Emeric Pressburger; *Director of Photography*: Ronald Neame; *Camera Operators*: Robert Krasker and Guy Green; *Film Editor*: David Lean; *Associate Editor*: Thelma Myers; *Special Effects*: F. Ford, Douglas Woolsey; *Sound Recordist*: C.C. Stevens; *Sound Supervisor*: A.W. Watkins;

Art Director: David Rawnsley; *Associate Director*: John Seabourne; *Production Secretary*: Joan Page;
Unit Manager: Sydney Streeter; *Technical Advisers*: M. Sluyser, James P. Power
Cast: Godfrey Tearle (Sir George Corbett), Eric Portman (Tom Earnshaw), Hugh Williams
(Frank Shelley), Bernard Miles (Geoff Hickman), Hugh Burden (John Glyn Haggard), Emrys
Jones (Bob Ashley), Pamela Brown (Els Meertens), Googie Withers (Jo de Vries), Joyce Redman
(Jet van Dierten), Hay Petrie (Burgomaster), Selma vaz Dias (Burgomaster's wife), Arnold
Marle (Pieter Sluys), Robert Helpmann (De Jong), Peter Ustinov (Priest), Alec Clunes
(Organist), Roland Culver (Naval Officer), Stewart Rome (Station Commander), James Carson
(Louis), Hector Abbas (Driver), Bill Akkerman (Willem), Joan Akkerman (Maartje), Peter
Schenke (Hendrik), Valerie Moon (Jannie), John Salew (Sentry), William D'Arcy (Officer),
David Ward, Robert Duncan (Airmen), Robert Beatty (Hopkins), Michael Powell (Despatching
Officer), John Longden (Ground Officer)

A British bomber crew returning from a raid on Stuttgart bails out over occupied
Holland. Aided by a friendly Dutch family, the men are taken to the local church
where they are helped by resistance worker Els Meertens, the local schoolteacher. The
Dutch network helps them to travel, disguised, across the occupied countryside, avoid-
ing the German patrols until, reaching the North Sea coast, they are hidden at the
house of Jo de Vries who – although the Germans believe she is loyal to them – is
working with the Allies. Under cover of an air raid, the crew escape by rowing boat,
finally making a landing on the newly situated 'lobster pots' – floating stages placed to
help grounded air crews waiting to be picked up by patrol vessels. Reaching England,
they prepare for their next bombing raid over Germany.

*The best non-documentary film that the war has inspired… no nonsense about Paladins of the
Air, but ordinary Englishmen resolutely doing a job as well as it can be done… Dialogue and acting, photography and direction, are similarly unostentatious and effective. Miss Pamela Brown
and Mr Eric Portman have the best chances and take them immensely well… Mr Michael Powell
and all his associates are to be congratulated on making a swell thriller which is also a message
of encouragement.*
New Statesman

*Lovely photography, first-class direction, straight forward production and sincere acting from peo-
ple who know their job put it at the top of its class so far. The story is based on fact… it is unique
in that it does not include the 'blonde bombshell' interest. The acting is so good that it is invidi-
ous to make distinctions. It is, in short, a film worth seeing with excellent propaganda value, and
is a credit to the British film industry.*
Monthly Film Bulletin

THE SILVER FLEET
(1943, 88 minutes, US: 81 minutes) The Archers/Rank.
Directors: Vernon Campbell Sewell and Gordon Wellesley; *Producers*: Michael Powell and Emeric
Pressburger; *Screenplay*: Vernon Campbell Sewell and Gordon Wellesley; *Production Design*: Alfred
Junge; *Director of Photography*: Erwin Hillier; *Film Editor*: Michael C. Chorlton; *Music Score*: Allan
Gray; *Sound Recording*: John Dennis and Desmond Dew; *Special Effects*: Eric Humphriss; *Camera
Operator*: Cyril Cooney; *Associate Producer*: Ralph Richardson; *Adviser*: M. Sluyser
Cast: Ralph Richardson (Jaap van Leyden), Googie Withers (Helene van Leyden), Esmond
Knight (von Schiffer), Beresford Egan (Krampf), John Longden (Jost Meertens), Kathleen Byron
(Schoolmistress), Frederick Burtwell (Captain Müller), Willem Akkerman (Willem van
Leyden), Charles Victor (Bastiaan Peters), Dorothy Gordon (Janni Peters), Joss Ambler
(Cornelis Smit), George Schelderup (Dirk), Margaret Emden (Bertha), Neville Mapp (Joop),

Ivor Barnard (Admiral), John Carol (Johann), Philip Leaver (Chief of Police), Laurence O'Madden (Captain Schneider), Anthony Eustrel (Lt Wernicke), Charles Minor (Bohme), Valentine Dyall (Markgraf), Lt Schouwenaar, RNN (U-Boat Captain), Lt van Dapperen, RNN (U-Boat Lieutenant), John Arnold (U-Boat Navigator) and personnel of the Royal Netherlands Navy

Dutch shipyard owner Jaap van Leyden is branded a Quisling when he collaborates with the occupying Nazi forces. Messages begin to appear from 'Piet Hein' – a legendary Dutch hero who had sunk the Spanish silver fleet off the coast of Cuba in 1628 – and a conspiracy grows among the workers. At trials of the first submarine, the Germans are overpowered and the vessel heads for England. Von Schiffer takes 30 hostages but van Leyden intervenes, and inviting the Nazi chiefs to his house, persuades them to attend trials for a second submarine. Helene van Leyden refuses to speak to her husband, believing him to be a traitor, and next morning he leaves a note explaining everything before leaving for the shipyard where he boards the submarine with the German chiefs. Once submerged, Van Leyden detonates an explosion killing all of the Nazis on board as well as himself.

Many fine qualities of direction, production and acting give this film a moving appeal which rises above the improbabilities of plot... Attention to detail makes the life of the little Dutch town and its people highly convincing... Much dramatic value is gained by the artistic use of periods of quiet and of half-light and night scenes, Ralph Richardson's is a fine restrained performance, as is that of Googie Withers as his wife.
Monthly Film Bulletin

This latest Archers production... is a sympathetically handled film, with a basically strong story, some arresting characterizations and a realistic flavour permeating it... Greatest obstacle which the film has to overcome is the 'choosiness' with which the paying public here now approaches films about the war.
Motion Picture Herald

THE LIFE AND DEATH OF COLONEL BLIMP
(US: Colonel Blimp)
(1943, 163 minutes, US: 148 minutes, Technicolor) The Archers/Rank.
Written, Produced and Directed: Michael Powell and Emeric Pressburger; *Director of Photography*: Georges Périnal; *Camera Operators*: Geoffrey Unsworth, Jack Cardiff, Harold Hayson; *Film Editor*: John Seabourne; *Assistant Editors*: Thelma Vyers, Peter Seabourne; *Process Shots*: W. Percy Day; *Technicolor Colour Control*: Natalie Kalmus; *Production Design*: Alfred Junge; *Make-up*: George Blackler, Dorrie Hamilton; *Music Score*: Allan Gray; *Sound Recording*: C.C. Stevens, Desmond Dew; *Production Manager*: Sydney Streeter; *Costume Design*: Joseph Bato; *Costumes*: Matilda Etches; *Military Adviser*: Lt General Sir Douglas Brownrigg; *Period Advisers*: E.F.E. Schoen, Dr C. Beard. *Management*: Sydney Streeter, Alec Saville; *Archers Secretary*: Joan Page; *Assistant Producer*: Richard Vernon; *Assistant Directors*: Ken Horne, Tom Payne; *Floor Manager*: Arthur Lawson
Cast: Anton Walbrook (Theo Kretschmar-Schuldorff), Roger Livesey (Clive Wynne Candy), Deborah Kerr (Edith Hunter/Barbara Wynn/Angela 'Johnny' Cannon), Roland Culver (Colonel Betteridge), Harry Welchman (Major Davis), Arthur Wontner (Embassy Counsellor), Albert Lieven (von Ritter), John Laurie (Murdoch), James McKechnie (Spud Wilson), Ursula Jeans (Frau von Kalteneck), Reginald Tate (Van Zijl), David Hutcheson (Hoppy), A.E. Matthews (President of the Tribunal), Carl Jaffe (von Reumann), Valentine Dyall (von Schonbron), Muriel Aked (Aunt Margaret), Felix Aylmer (Bishop), Neville Mapp (Stuffy Graves), Robert Harris (Embassy Secretary), Frith Banbury (Babyface Fitzroy), Vincent Holman (Club Porter, 1942),

Spencer Trevor (Period Blimp), Dennis Arundell (Cafe Orchestra Leader), James Knight (Club Porter, 1902), David Ward (Kaunitz), Eric Maturin (Colonel Goodhead), Count Zichy (Colonel Berg), Jan van Loewen (Indignant Citizen), Jane Millican (Nurse Erna), Phyllis Morris (Pebble), Diana Marshall (Sybil), Captain W.H. Barrett (Texan), Corporal Thomas Palmer (Sergeant), Yvonne Andrée (Nun), Marjorie Gresley (Matron), Helen Debroy (Mrs Wynne), Norman Pierce (Mr Wynne), Edward Cooper (BBC official), Joan Swinstead (Secretary), Wally Patch, Ferdy Mayne, John Varley, Patrick MacNee.

1943. Enterprising young Lieutenant 'Spud' Wilson 'captures' Major Clive Wynne Candy and his men at a Turkish Bath in London six hours before the agreed start of a Home Guard exercise, insisting that rules can no longer be observed in modern warfare. The outraged Candy lambasts the younger man for his impudence, reminding him that one day he will be an old man too.

Candy's own story is told in flashback. During the Boer War of 1902 he rashly travels to Berlin with English governess Edith Hunter to confront German propagandist Kaunitz. Candy is challenged to a duel in which both he and his opponent, Theo Kretschmar-Schuldorff, are taken injured to a nursing home. They become friends, and when Edith announces her engagement to Theo, Clive realizes too late that he is in love with her.

The First World War, and Colonel Candy's British troops adhere to the honourable fighting methods of his Boer campaigns. Marrying Barbara, a war nurse who bears a striking resemblance to Edith, Clive learns that Theo is a prisoner-of-war in England. The proud Theo shuns him but later telephones and the two old friends meet again.

The Second World War finds Theo a German refugee in England escaping from Nazi rule. He meets the widowed Clive who is no longer required by the War Office because of his outmoded ideas. Theo and 'Johnny', Clive's driver, persuade him to join the Home Guard, but with the spoiling of the exercise Candy fears that his methods no longer have anything to offer. Theo comforts him, convincing him that modern war needs new ideas and that the British soldier is still the greatest in the world.

The turkish bath sequence is shown at the beginning of the picture as well as at the end. This device is unjustified, especially in a picture that runs for $2\frac{3}{4}$ hours. There is much on the credit side, however. Roger Livesey is thoroughly likeable as Clive Candy. He 'ages' astonishingly well. Anton Walbrook is at his best as the German. Deborah Kerr is delightful in the three roles... Michael Powell and Emeric Pressburger... have maintained their high standard of dialogue and direction.
Evening Standard

This is a consistently entertaining film, nowhere boring and yet hardly anywhere satisfactory as a piece of narrative or a piece of fiction... Miss Kerr is seen throughout as various young women, all of them remarkably alike and remarkably pretty and articulate. Mr Walbrook has more than one occasion for long speeches and delivers them with gentle pathos and charm, and Mr Roger Livesey's bluff, likeable Blimp is a jolly tour de force of character acting. The film's Technicolor for which the French expert Georges Périnal is responsible, is the showiest and least aggressive we have seen.
Manchester Guardian

Here is an excellent film whose basic story could have been told within usual feature limits, but which, instead, is extended close to 3 hours. Longer or shorter, this panorama of British army life is depicted with a technical skill and artistry that marks it as one of the really fine pix to come

out of a British studio... Title is based on the symbolic figure of old-time English officers who have been axed, not only due to age but because of their contempt for present methods of warfare as compared with the 'good old days'.
Variety

THE VOLUNTEER

(1943, 46 minutes) The Archers.
Written, Produced and Directed: Michael Powell and Emeric Pressburger; *Production Manager:* Sydney Streeter; *Director of Photography:* Freddie Ford; *Film Editor:* John Seabourne; *Production Designer:* Alfred Junge; *Music Score:* Allan Gray; *Sound Recording:* Desmond Dew
Cast: Ralph Richardson (Himself), Pat McGrath (Fred Davey), Michael Powell, Laurence Olivier, Anna Neagle, Herbert Wilcox

Following a performance in the title role of *Othello* at the New Theatre, Ralph Richardson is approached by his dresser Fred Davey, asking if he will sign an autograph for his girlfriend. Next day, Fred tells Ralph that he has joined the Fleet Air Arm and will no longer be able to work for him. Fred becomes a hero, rescuing a pilot from a blazing plane on the deck of an aircraft carrier, and receives his medal at Buckingham Palace where Ralph requests an autograph for his girlfriend (his daughter).

A CANTERBURY TALE

(1944, 124 minutes, US: 95 minutes) The Archers.
Written, Produced and Directed Michael Powell and Emeric Pressburger; *Production Manager:* George Maynard; *Director of Photography:* Erwin Hillier; *Film Editor:* John Seabourne; *Production Designer:* Alfred Junge; *Music Score:* Allan Gray; *Music Director:* Walter Goehr; *Sound Recording:* C.C. Stevens, Desmond Dew; *Exteriors Recording:* Alan Whatley; *Period Adviser:* Herbert Norris; *Production Manager:* George Maynard; *Assistant Director:* George R. Busby
Cast: Eric Portman (Thomas Colpepper, JP), Sheila Sim (Alison Smith), Dennis Price (Peter Gibbs), Sgt John Sweet (Bob Johnson), Esmond Knight (Narrator/Seven Sisters Soldier/Village Idiot), Charles Hawtrey (Thomas Duckett), Hay Petrie (Woodcock), George Merritt (Ned Horton), Edward Rigby (Jim Horton), Freda Jackson (Prudence Honeywood), Betty Jardine (Fee Baker), Eliot Makeham (Organist),

● The main cast (apart from Eric Portman) of *A Canterbury Tale*. From left: Dennis Price, Esmond Knight, Sgt John Sweet, Sheila Sim and Graham Moffat – insolent fat boy of many Will Hay comedies, seen here in one of his less demanding roles.

Harvey Golden (Sgt Roczinsky), Leonard Smith (Leslie), James Tamsitt (Terry), David Todd (David), Beresford Egan (PC Overden), Anthony Holles (Sgt Bassett), Maude Lambert (Miss Grainger), Wally Bosco (ARP Warden), Charles Paton (Ernie Brooks), Jane Millican (Susanna Foster), John Slater (Sgt Len), Michael Golden (Sgt Smale), Graham Moffatt (Sgt 'Stuffy'), Esma Cannon (Agnes), Mary Line (Leslie's mother), Winifred Swaffer (Mrs Horton), Michael Howard

(Archie), Judith Furse (Dorothy Bird), Barbara Waring (Polly Finn), Jean Shepheard (Gwladys Swinton), Margaret Scudamore (Mrs Colpepper), Joss Ambler (Police Inspector), Jessie James (Waitress), Kathleen Lucas (Passer-by), H.F. Maltby (Mr Portal), Eric Maturin (Geoffrey's father), Parry Jones (Arthur) [US: Kim Hunter (Bob's fiancée), Raymond Massey (narrator)]

Three train passengers arrive during a black-out at Chillingbourne in Kent and, as they make their way through the village, Alison Smith has something poured on to her hair by an unseen attacker. At the town hall they learn that she is the eleventh victim of the mysterious 'glueman'. Magistrate Thomas Colpepper arranges for Bob Johnson – an American soldier who had intended to get out at Canterbury – to stay at a local guest house and hopes that he will stay to see more of the country, although Bob is anxious to move on.

Alison, Bob and Peter Gibbs attend Colpepper's lecture next day on the history of the Pilgrims Way and the surrounding area. Moved by the talk, Alison later revisits the scene of a pre-war caravanning holiday spent with her fiancé, now missing in action. There she meets Colpepper, who finds that she too has a love of the countryside, though for different reasons. Unseen, they overhear Bob and Peter discussing their lives before the war and their suspicions of the 'glueman's' identity.

On the train next morning, Colpepper admits that he is the glueman, but claims his intention was to drive girls to his lectures where they might learn the importance of their national heritage instead of going out with GIs while their sweethearts are away. Peter determines to report him on their arrival, but Colpepper insists that he will receive his own judgement.

At Canterbury Bob hears that his girl has enlisted in the WACs and receives several letters telling him all is well. Alison visits the blacksmith where her caravan is stored and learns that her fiancé has been found alive in Gibraltar, while Peter – a classical music student who was forced to take work in peace time as a cinema organist – realizes his ambition to play the organ inside Canterbury Cathedral during a service for the departing troops. All have received their blessings save Colpepper, who must serve his penance alone.

Sincerity and simplicity shine through every foot of this oversized modern version of Chaucer's epic tale. Here is rare beauty… First honors go to Erwin Hillier, whose camerawork is superb. Nothing more effective by way of a time transition shot has been conceived than the way he carries his audience through nine centuries in a few seconds.
Variety

Because they represent the only consistent unification of script, production and direction in British films, Michael Powell and Emeric Pressburger arouse expectancy and generally arrive at something different and individual. Their besetting weakness – lack of coherent purpose in their stories – is more pronounced than ever in this their latest product… This murky, unexciting mystery is unravelled by the three pilgrims, a British soldier, a land girl, and most emphatically Sergeant John Sweet of the US Army. He is an untrained actor discovered by Michael Powell and he is vividly alive and solid in a world that slips by hazily like a dream.
News Chronicle

I think I have never seen the spirit of young England… so exquisitely caught as it is in these Kentish landscapes, in those white clouds sailing, in the immemorial smithies, the immensity of the great cathedral… This is the corner of earth for which men die, pictured with consummate artistry and brilliant understanding. The acting… is beyond reproach. Not so the strange mentality of Mr

Michael Powell and Mr Emeric Pressburger, who have lavished their talents, created and thrown away a thing of great beauty, for this preposterous, this silly story...
Sunday Chronicle

At a time when everybody's nerves are on edge, A Canterbury Tale *is as good as a day in the country... I carried away from [it] an enjoyment that I was loath to examine too closely.*
William Whitebait, New Statesman

I KNOW WHERE I'M GOING!

(1945, 91 minutes) The Archers.

Written, Produced and Directed: Michael Powell and Emeric Pressburger; *Director of Photography:* Erwin Hillier; *Camera Operator:* Cecil Cooney; *Art Director:* Alfred Junge; *Film Editor:* John Seabourne; *Special Effects:* Henry Harris; *Music Score:* Allan Gray; *Music Director:* Walter Goehr; *Sound Recordist:* C.C. Stevens; *Assistant Producer:* George Busby; *Assistant Director:* John Tunstall; *Special Effects:* Henry Harris; *Gaelic Adviser:* Malcolm MacKellaig; *Ceilidh Adviser:* John Laurie; *Sound Effects:* Members of the Glasgow Orpheus Choir

Cast: Wendy Hiller (Joan Webster), Roger Livesey (Torquil MacNeil), Pamela Brown (Catriona), Finlay Currie (Ruairidh Mor), Murdo Morrison (Kenny), Ian Sadler (Ian), Capt C.W.R. Knight (Colonel Barnstaple). George Carney (Mr Webster), Walter Hudd (Hunter), Capt Duncan MacKechnie (Cpt 'Lochinvar'), Margot Fitzsimmons (Bridie), Donald Strachan (Shepherd), John Rae (Old shepherd), Duncan MacIntyre (His son), Jean Cadell (Postmistress), Norman Shelley (Sir Robert Bellinger), Ivy Milton (Peigi), Anthony Eustrel (Hooper), Petula Clark (Cheril), Alec Faversham (Martin), Catherine Lacey (Mrs Robinson), Valentine Dyall (Mr Robinson), Nancy Price (Mrs Crozier), Herbert Lomas (Mr Campbell), John Laurie (John Campbell), Kitty Kirwan (Mrs Campbell), Graham Moffatt (RAF Sergeant), Boyd Stevens, Maxwell Kennedy, Jean Houston Members of Glasgow Orpheus Choir (Ceilidh Singers), Arthur Chesney (Harmonica Player), 'Mr Ramshaw' (Torquil, the Eagle)

Stubborn, spoilt Joan Webster journeys north to marry wealthy Sir Robert Bellinger on the Scottish island of Kiloran, but a thick fog prevents her from leaving the mainland. Naval Lieutenant Torquil MacNeil suggests she spend the night at the house of his friend Catriona Potts. Next day the fog is replaced by a fierce gale, which again prevents a crossing. Torquil and Joan move to the Tobermory Hotel, on the way passing Castle Moy to which entry is forbidden to the Lairds of Kiloran by an ancient curse on the family. Torquil admits he is the penniless owner of Kiloran, forced to rent the island to Bellinger in order to pay the bills.

Still marooned, the pair attend a wedding anniversary ceilidh where it becomes clear that Torquil is in love with Joan, who, for the first time, is unsure of her feelings. She bribes young Kenny to take to sea in appalling weather but Torquil – concerned for Kenny's safety – takes command of the boat himself and by his skill and strength saves them from being lost in the treacherous Corryvreckan whirlpool.

Next day, Joan finally sets off for Kiloran as Torquil enters the forbidden Castle Moy. He learns the true nature of the legend as Joan returns to fulfil the prophesy: any MacNeil who enters shall not leave there a free man, but be chained to a woman for the rest of his days...

I Know Where I'm Going! *doesn't even try to be a great movie, but it is a very good one in its charming, unpretentious way.*
Time

Once again those gifted collaborators Messrs Powell and Pressburger are to be congratulated on

proving that British films, in quality, if not quantity, are pre-eminent.
Standard

I Know Where I'm Going! *has excellent qualities, marred a little by the awkwardness we know so well... the story is a guileless little affair... designed to give depth to the scenery of the Scottish Isles, and this is, believe me, landscape and seascape with a vengeance... Miss Wendy Hiller and Mr Sam* (sic) *Livesey behave very nicely and naturally in the foreground, and in Capt C.W.R. Knight, the naturalist, there is discovered a screen personality of roaring charm.*
New Statesman

A MATTER OF LIFE AND DEATH

(US: Stairway To Heaven)
(1946, 104 minutes) Technicolor. A Production of The Archers.
Written, Produced and Directed: Michael Powell and Emeric Pressburger;
Director of Photography: Jack Cardiff; *Camera Operator:* Geoffrey Unsworth; *Motorbike shots*: Michael Chorlton; *Film Editor:* Reginald Mills; *Special Effects*: Douglas Woolsey, Henry Harris and Technicolor Ltd; *Additional Effects*: W. Percy Day; *Production Designer*: Alfred Junge; *Technicolor Colour Control*: Natalie Kalmus; *Associate*: Joan Bridge; *Assistant Art Director:* Arthur Lawson; *Costume Designer:* Hein Heckroth; *Music Score*: Allan Gray; *Conductor:* Walter Goehr; *Assistant Conductor*: W.L. Williamson; *Liaison Editor*: John Seabourne Jnr; *Make-up*: George Blackler; *Hair Styles*: Ida Mills; *Sound Recordist*: C.C. Stevens; *Associate Producer*: George R. Busby; *Assistant Director*: Parry Jones, Jnr
Cast: David Niven (Peter Carter), Roger Livesey (Frank Reeves), Raymond Massey (Abraham Farlan), Kim Hunter (June), Marius Goring (Conductor 71), Abraham Sofaer (Judge), Robert Coote (Bob Trubshawe), Joan Maude (Recorder), Kathleen Byron (Angel), Bonar Colleano (US Pilot), Edwin Max (Dr McEwen), Richard Attenborough (Pilot), Bob Roberts (Dr Gaertler), Robert Atkins (Vicar), Betty Potter (Mrs Tucker), John Longden (Narrator), Robert Arden, Wally Patch, Tom Duggan, Roger Snowden, Joan Verney, Wendy Thompson

Returning from a bombing raid, Peter Carter makes radio contact with June at a US air base on England's south coast before jumping – without a parachute – from the flaming wreckage of his plane over the English Channel. Somehow surviving and being washed ashore, Peter meets June cycling across the sands and realizes that fate has brought them together.

In the 'Other World', it becomes clear that Peter has been 'missed' in the thick fog. Conductor 71 is despatched to explain the error and to bring him back less than alive. Carter refuses to return, arguing that, as he has fallen in love, he now has everything to live for. June consults Dr Frank Reeves over Peter's attempts to explain the 'Other World' to her. The Conductor returns – visible only to Peter – to advise that an appeal has been granted. Reeves, aware of the significance of these 'hallucinations' to his patient, arranges an emergency operation on the night that the 'appeal' is to take place but is killed in a crash with the approaching ambulance before the operation/appeal takes place. In the Other World, Peter chooses Frank as his counsel and Reeves, Trubshawe and the Conductor return to earth seeking to support their case, finally securing June's tear drop as their only piece of hard evidence.

The trial begins, with fiercely anti-British Abraham Farlan as prosecutor. Farlan is a skilful advocate, but Reeves insists on fairness for his client. Finally the entire court descends the mammoth staircase to earth where they question Peter and June. Frank tricks her into thinking that she must sacrifice her own life to save Peter's and as she steps on to the ascending stairway, the case is won and the Judge agrees a new life span for Peter. The operation is a success, and Peter and June look forward to a new life together.

A brilliant experiment which will be enjoyed by many and appreciated by only a few.
Monthly Film Bulletin

Michael Powell and Emeric Pressburger... have a reputation for eschewing the conventional approach to cinema. As a result, each of their films has tended to create a minor sensation among cineastes, although in perspective they cannot be assessed as anything more than rather mediocre curiosities... there is no virtue in just being 'out of step' and it is time that [they] achieved something more than mere oddity.
Humphrey Swingler, Our Time

Yet... the film has astonishing merits... I don't believe that by any stretching of critical kindness can A Matter of Life and Death *be described as a good film; yet it is not boring, and not undramatic. Everything is at odds, except purely cinematic skill...*
New Statesman

BLACK NARCISSUS

(1947, 100 minutes) Technicolor. The Archers.
Written, Produced and Directed: Michael Powell and Emeric Pressburger; *Screenplay:* based on the novel by Rumer Godden; *Director of Photography:* Jack Cardiff; *Camera Operators:* Ted Scaife, Stan Sayers; *Film Editor:* Reginald Mills; *Process Shots:* W. Percy Day; *Technicolor Colour Control:* Natalie Kalmus; *Associate:* Joan Bridge; *Production Designer:* Alfred Junge; *Assistant Art Director:* Arthur Lawson; *Costumes:* Hein Heckroth; *Music and Sound Score:* composed and conducted by Brian Easdale, with the London Symphony Orchestra; *Sound Recordist:* Stanley Lambourne; *Dubbing:* Gordon K. McCallum; *Associate Producer:* George R. Busby; *Assistant Director:* Sydney Streeter
Cast: Deborah Kerr (Sister Clodagh), David Farrar (Mr Dean), Sabu (Dilip Rai, The Young General), Flora Robson (Sister Philippa), Esmond Knight (The Old General), Jean Simmons (Kanchi), Kathleen Byron (Sister Ruth), Jenny Laird (Sister Blanche [Honey]), Judith Furse (Sister Briony), May Hallatt (Angu Ayah), Shaun Noble (Con), Eddie Whaley Jnr (Joseph Anthony), Nancy Roberts (Mother Dorothea), Ley On (Phuba)

Sister Clodagh is sent to establish a convent high in the Himalayas, and takes four sisters with her to help set up a school and dispensary: Philippa, Briony, Blanche and the troublesome Ruth. English agent Mr Dean warns that the project is doomed to failure, predicting that they will leave before the rains break. Convent routine is quickly upset when Young General Dilip Rai arrives seeking to be taught at the 'girls only' school. Dean then deposits a wild and exotic young girl Kanchi who also joins the classes.

The howling winds and oppressive atmosphere distract the nuns from their purpose. Ruth becomes aware of perfume in the air – 'Black Narcissus', worn by the Young General – and Philippa plants flowers instead of the vegetables they will need. Even Clodagh's thoughts wander back to recall her youth and the man she loved many years before. On Dean's advice, Sister Briony refuses to see a seriously ill boy, but the kindhearted Blanche treats the child who later dies. The villagers shun the sisters, holding them responsble for his death. Dilip Rai now runs away with Kanchi, and Dean warns Clodagh that they must all leave before anything else happens.

Giving up her vows, Ruth flees the convent for Dean's house where she declares her love for him. Dean rejects her and, after a hysterical outburst, she returns to the convent and – now deranged – attempts to push Sister Clodagh from the cliff, but instead falls to her own death. Defeated, Clodagh and the remaining sisters prepare to

● On the set of *Black Narcissus* (1947). From left: Deborah Kerr, Emeric Pressburger, author
Rumer Godden, Michael Powell and art director 'Uncle Alfred' Junge.

return to Calcutta. As Dean bids Clodagh a melancholy farewell, the rains break as he
had predicted.

*The best film Michael Powell and Emeric Pressburger have given us... the most satisfying to the
eye, the most human, the most consistent. Their work is always stimulating and lovely to look at...
a story absorbing in itself, skilfully told and acted against scenes of sheer enchantment.*
Daily Telegraph

*There is little doubt that audiences, appreciative of the finer points of film making will enjoy this
Archers production. The photography is among the best Technicolor yet seen on American screens..
There is plenty of room left for doubt, however, whether Mr and Mrs Smith, USA, will be able
quite to comprehend the motions behind the actions in this picture. In any case, its appeal will be
greater for women than for men.*
Motion Picture Herald

Cynics may dub this lavish production Brief Encounter in the Himalayas... *The production
and camerawork atone for minor lapses in the story, Jack Cardiff's photography being outstanding. Most effective acting comes from Kathleen Byron, who has the picture's plum as the neurotic
half-crazed Sister Ruth.*
Variety

THE END OF THE RIVER
(1947, 83 minutes US: 80 minutes) The Archers.
Director: Derek Twist; *Producers:* Michael Powell and Emeric Presburger; *Screenplay:* Wolfgang
Wilhelm, based on the novel by Desmond Holdridge; *Director of Photography:* Christopher Challis;
Art Director: Fred Pusey; *Assistant Art Director:* E.E.C. Scott; *Production Manager:* John Alderson; *Film*

Editor: Brereton Porter; *Assistant Editor*: David Powell; *Music Score*: Lambert Williamson; *Sound Recordist*: Charles Knott; *Dubbing*: Gordon K. McCullum; *Associate Producer*: George R. Busby; *Assistant Director*: Geoffrey Lambert

Cast: Sabu (Manoel), Bibi Férriera (Teresa), Esmond Knight (Dantos), Robert Douglas (Jones), Torin Thatcher (Lisboa), Antoinette Cellier (Conceicao), Orlando Martins (Harrigan), Raymond Lovell (Porpino), James Hayter (Chico), Nicolette Bernard (Dona Serafina), Minto Cato (Dona Paula), Maurice Denham (Defending Counsel), Eva Hudson (Maria Gonsalves), Alan Wheatley (Iryogen), Charles Hawtrey (Raphael), Zena Marshall (Sante), Dennis Arundell (Continho), Milton Rosmer (Judge), Peter Illing (Ship's Agent), Nino Rossini (Feliciano), Basil Appleby (Ship's Officer), Milo Sperber (Ze), Andreas Malandrinos (Officer of the Indian Protection Society), Arthur Goullet (Pedlar), Russell Napier (Padre)

Cut off from his family, Manoel is sent to a slave camp run by Cypriano Dantos, where he meets and falls in love with Teresa. The slaves are treated badly and many die of disease; Dantos himself becomes a victim of beri-beri. Lisboa leads the survivors to Belem do Para where they find new jobs and better conditions. Manoel and Teresa marry and join Lisboa working a passenger steam boat along the river.

During a trip ashore, Manoel falls in with Tryogen and enrols with the revolutionary Brotherhood of Maritime Workers who find him work, but he is later blacklisted when the corrupt union is discredited. Eventually offered a job at the docks, he is involved in a brawl and kills a man. Defence counsel pleads for mercy, claiming Manoel's crime is the result of his innocence of the ways of the white man – 'The twig in the current has travelled a long way – who is guilty? the twig or the current?' Released, Manoel returns with Chico and Teresa to his simple life at the end of the river.

This is an unusual production, but a monotonous series of flashbacks break the even development of the plot and it is difficult at times to keep track of the characters around whom the story is built. The result is that interest is lost and the film becomes boring. It is a pity, also, that so little use has been made of the South American river scenery. Bibi Férreira gives character and charm to the role of Teresa and Sabu arouses sympathy for the bewildered boy Manoel.
Monthly Film Bulletin

THE RED SHOES

(1948, 136 minutes) Technicolor. The Archers.
Written, Produced and Directed: Michael Powell and Emeric Pressburger; *Original Screenplay:* Emeric Pressburger; *Additional Dialogue:* Keith Winter; *Director of Photography*: Jack Cardiff; *Camera Operator*: Christopher Challis; *Special Photographic Effects*: F. George Dunn and D. Hague; *Technicolor Colour Control*: Natalie Kalmus; *Associate*: Joan Bridge; *Film Editor*: Reginald Mills; *Production Designer*: Hein Heckroth; *Scenic Artist*: Alfred Roberts; *Special Painting*: Ivor Beddoes, Jozef Natanson; *Music Score*: Brian Easdale; Ted Heath's Kenny Baker Swing Group; *Sound Recordist*: Charles Poulton; *Dubbing*: Gordon K. MacCullum; *Music*: recorded by Ted Drake; *Liaison Editor*: John Seabourne Jnr; *Art Director*: Arthur Lawson; *Continuity*: Doreen North; *Wardrobe*: Dorothy Edwards; *Miss Shearer's dresses*: Jacques Fath of Paris, Mattli of London; *Mlle Tcherina's dresses*: Carven of Paris; *Assistant Producer*: George R. Busby; *Assistant Director:* Sydney Streeter
The Red Shoes ballet: *Choreography*: Robert Helpmann; the part of the Shoemaker created and danced by Léonide Massine; *Music*: composed by Brian Easdale and performed by the Royal Philharmonic Orchestra conducted by Sir Thomas Beecham; *Solo dancer and Assistant Maitre-de-Ballet*: Alan Carter; *Solo dancer and Assistant Maitresse-de-Ballet*: Joan Harris
Cast: Anton Walbrook (Boris Lermontov), Marius Goring (Julian Craster), Moira Shearer (Victoria

● **An over-leggy ad for The Archers greatest success, *The Red Shoes* – 'a dancing, singing, swinging love tale' makes it sound like a Tommy Steele picture.**

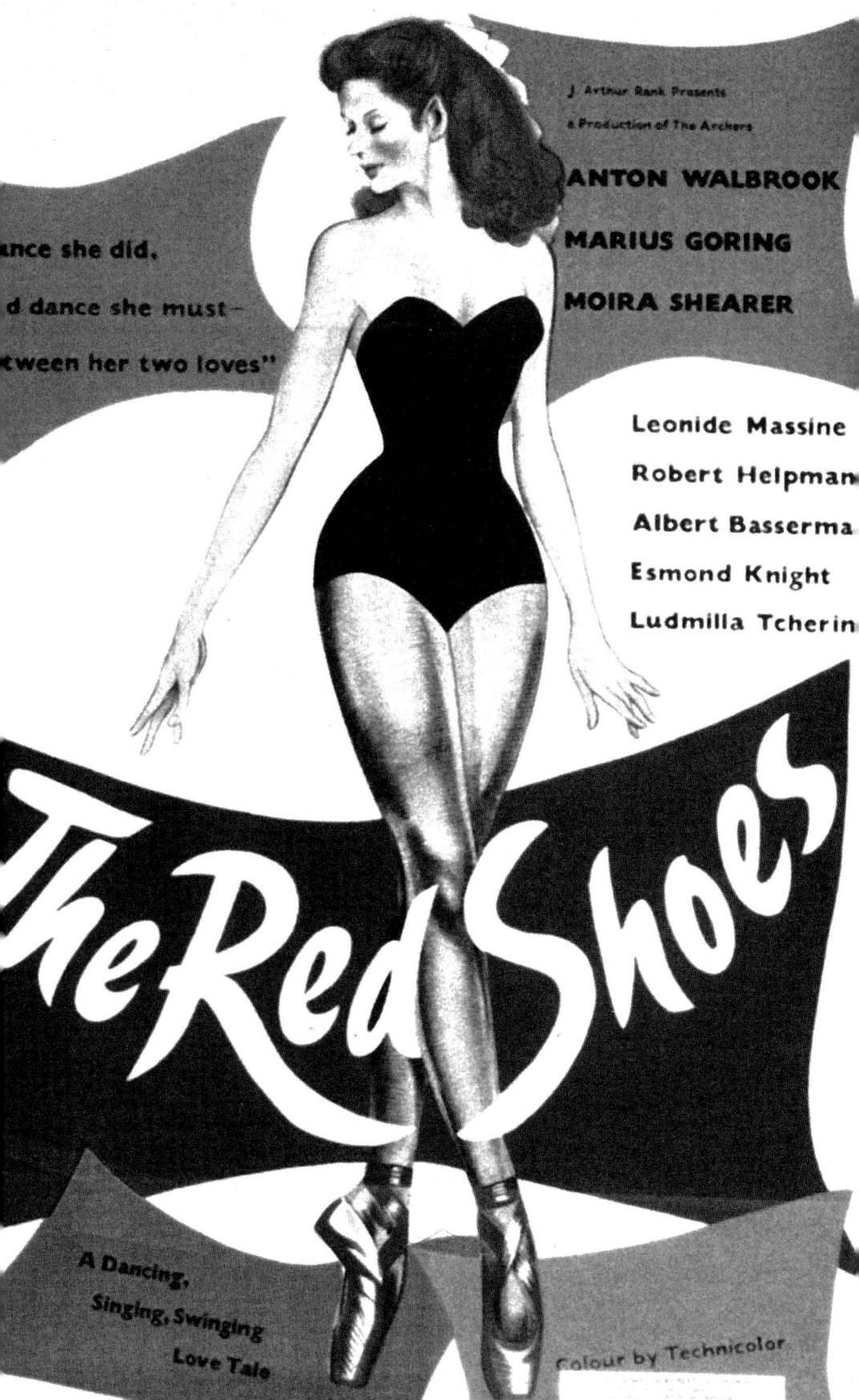

Page), Robert Helpmann (Ivan Boleslawsky), Léonide Massine (Ljubov), Albert Basserman (Ratov), Ludmilla Tcherina (Irina Boronskaja), Esmond Knight (Livy), Austin Trevor (Professor Palmer), Eric Berry (Dimitri), Irene Browne (Lady Neston), Derek Elphinstone (Lord Oldham), Madame Rambert (Herself), Jerry Verno (Stage Door Keeper), Joy Rawlins (Gladys, Victoria's friend), Jean Short (Terry), Gordon Littman (Ike), Marcel Poncin (M Boudin), Hay Petrie (Boisson), Julia Lang (Balletomane), Bill Shine (Her companion), Yvonne Andre (Victoria's dresser), George Woodbridge (Doorman)

After meeting Victoria Page at a reception, ballet impresario Boris Lermontov invites her to Covent Garden, where she is accepted as a member of the *corps-de-ballet*. A young composer, Julian Craster, is engaged to work on a new ballet based on the Hans Christian Andersen fairy-tale *The Red Shoes.*

Lermontov – who believes that nothing is more important than to dance – is furious when prima ballerina Irina Boronskaja leaves the company to be married, and in Monte Carlo, tells Vicky that she is to dance *The Red Shoes*. The new ballet is a great success and Vicky an overnight star, but during the long weeks of close rehearsal she and Julian have fallen in love. When Lermontov dismisses the composer, Vicky leaves the company and marries Julian in London.

A year later, Vicky is holidaying in Monte Carlo when Lermontov asks her to dance The Red Shoes again, hoping to lure her back to the company. On the night of her performance, Julian arrives and they quarrel. Forced to choose between ballet and her husband, Vicky tells Julian that she must dance but, preparing for her entrance, she is driven to run away. Hurtling from the theatre, she falls from the balcony under an approaching train. As in the fairy-tale, the Red Shoes have danced her to her death. Inside the theatre, Lermontov announces the tragedy to a stunned audience, and the ballet is performed in her honour, a single spotlight now tracing her steps around the stage.

The Red Shoes could have been a masterpiece... [but Vicky's] final suicide is so incredible that one cannot take it seriously... As for the final shots of her bleeding to death in Glorious Technicolor, these drag the film down to the level of Duel in the Sun... *Nevertheless, the artists responsible for this film deserve our gratitude for aiming high; and their success is sufficient to make this a film not be missed.*
Fernau Hall, New Theatre

The particular and startling merit of the film is that for some twenty minutes it gives us a ballet which will surely be remembered as the first which was at once worthy of the title, and not borrowed by the cinema from the stage... a thing of beauty. Miss Shearer has shown us, at Covent Garden, that she is a lovely dancer: in this film-ballet she seems more magical still. The film audience, at any rate, were quite overcome; they actually interrupted the film with their applause – and that, as every film-goer knows, happens rarely in the cinema.
Manchester Guardian

For the first 60 minutes, this is a common place backstage melodrama, in which temperamental ballerinas replace the more conventional showgirls. Then a superb ballet.. is staged with breathtaking beauty, out-classing anything that could be done on the stage.. Although the story may be trite, there are many compensations, notably the flawless performance of Anton Walbrook, whose interpretation... is one of the best things he has done on screen.
Variety

THE SMALL BACK ROOM

(US: Hour of Glory)

(1949, 108 minutes, US: 97 minutes) A Production of The Archers for London Films.
Written, Produced and Directed: Michael Powell and Emeric Pressburger; *Screenplay*: Emeric
Pressburger, based on the novel by Nigel Balchin; *Director of Photography:* Christopher Challis;
Camera Operator: Freddie Francis; *Supervising Editor*: Reginald Mills; *Film Editor*: Clifford Turner;
Production Designer: Hein Heckroth; *Dress Designer*: Josephine Boss; *Art Director*: John Hoesli; *Music
Score*: Brian Easdale; *Additional Music* (night-club sequence): Ted Heath's Kenny Baker Swing
Group and Fred Lewis; *Sound Recordist*: Alan Allen; *Dubbing*: Bill Sweeny; *Continuity*: Doreen
North; *Assistant Producer*: George R. Busby; *Assistant Director*: Sydney Streeter
Cast: David Farrar (Sammy Rice), Kathleen Byron (Susan), Jack Hawkins (R. B. Waring), Leslie
Banks (Colonel Holland), Michael Gough (Stuart), Cyril Cusack (Corporal Taylor), Milton
Rosmer (Professor Mair), Michael Goodliffe (Till), Emrys Jones (Joe), Anthony Bushell
(Strang), Renee Asherson (ATS Corporal), Walter Fitzgerald (Brine), James Dale (Brigadier),
Geoffrey Keen (Pinker), Sam Kydd (Crowhurst), Sidney James (Knucksie), James Carney (Sgt
Groves), Henry Caine (Sgt Major Rose), Elwyn Brook-Jones (Gladwin), June Elvin (Gillian),
David Hutcheson (Norval), Roderick Lovell (Pearson), Roddy Hughes (Doctor), Bryan Forbes
(Peterson), Robert Morley (Minister)

Research scientist Sammy Rice suffers agonies with an artifical foot but, to please
Susan, he resists the urge to drown the pain in whisky. While assigned to help Captain
Stuart make safe a new booby trap device causing many casualties, he goes against
Professor Mair and R.B. Waring who are trying to 'sell' an unsuitable new gun to the
army. Mair leaves the section, and Susan is furious when Rice hesitates to apply for the
job. She walks out, leaving him to drink himself into a stupor. A telephone call arouses
him and he heads for Dorset but on arrival learns that Stuart has been killed attempt-
ing to defuse one of the devices. With clues supplied by Stuart's notes, Sammy tackles
the second bomb and finally makes it safe, discovering the secret of its mechanism as
he does so.

Back in London, Sammy is told by Colonel Holland that a new army unit is to be
set up and that he is to be allowed a free hand over staff and operations. Recovering his
self confidence, he is reunited with Susan and they return home together.

*I have a theory that when the heroes of Nigel Balchin's novels are about fifteen a girl dares them
to dive off a high board and they are afraid to do so. By the time they are old enough to be a
character in one of [his] books they have become bad-tempered neurotics who bully their women,
torment themselves and can only achieve a measure of salvation by carrying out a feat of extreme
daring... This is one of the best films the Powell-Pressburger team have made, and a certainty in
due course for a list of the year's best.*
Daily Mail

*Few film producers seem to realise that if you want to make a good film a good script is the pri-
mary essential. Most of them, indeed, shy away from the fact as if it were something unsavoury.
Still, perhaps, they don't want to make a good film – possibly they think you don't want to see
one. If you do though, you can see* The Small Back Room. *It is the latest and, I consider, the
best production of Michael Powell and Emeric Pressburger.*
Graphic

*Where would British films be just now without Powell and Pressburger? Precious and prolific,
stylish and commercial, intelligent and popular, these two are beyond question the live wires of
the day. Greater artists we have, but not turning out pictures often enough to liven the dreary*

prospects on our screens. Whatever one likes or dislikes in a P & P picture – and for myself I have never liked the whole of one – at least they are never boring, ugly or banal. And that is much to be able to say.

Time and Tide

GONE TO EARTH

(US: The Wild Heart)

(1950, 110 minutes; US: 82 minutes) Technicolor. A Production of The Archers. London Films/Vanguard Productions.

Written, Produced and Directed: Michael Powell and Emeric Pressburger; *Presented:* by Alexander Korda and David O. Selznick; *Screenplay:* based on the novel by Mary Webb; *Director of Photography*: Christopher Challis; *Camera Operator:* Freddie Francis; *Film Editor:* Reginald Mills; *Process Shots*: W. Percy Day; *Technicolor Colour Consultant*: Joan Bridge; *Production Designer:* Hein Heckroth; *Art Director*: Arthur Lawson; *Assistant Designer:* Ivor Beddoes; *Music Score*: Brian Easdale, with the Boyd Neel Orchestra; *Sound Recordist:* Charles Poulton, John Cox; *Animals supplied by*: Captain C.W.R. Knight. *Animals trained by*: Jean Knight; *Assistant Producer:* George R. Busby; *Assistant Director:* Sydney Streeter US: *Additional Direction:* Rouben Mamoulian

Cast: Jennifer Jones (Hazel Woodus), David Farrar (Squire Jack Reddin), Cyril Cusack (Edward Marston), Sybil Thorndike (Mrs Marston), Esmond Knight (Abel Woodus), Edward Chapman (Mr James), Hugh Griffith (Andrew Vessons), George Cole (Albert), Beatrice Varley (Aunt Prowde), Frances Clare (Amelia Clomber), Valentine Dunn (Martha), Bartlett Mullins, Arthur Reynolds, Gerald Lawson, Raymond Rollett (Chapel Elders), Richard Nairne (Martha's Brother), Gerald Lawson (Roadmender), Owen Holder (Brother Minister), Peter Dunlop (Cornet Player), Raymond Rollett (Landlord, Hunter's Arms), Anne Tetheradge (Miss James), Louis Phillips (Policeman), Daniel Stephens (Master of Fox Hounds) [US: Joseph Cotten (Narrator)]

1897. Shropshire girl Hazel Woodus lives with her father Abel and Foxy, a half-tame fox rescued from the hated foxhounds, her life ruled by the superstitions of her dead mother. Walking late one night, she believes herself pursued by the 'Black Huntsman' and accepts a lift from Squire Reddin who takes her to his home at Undern Manor and attempts to seduce her. Hazel escapes with the help of the squire's manservant Andrew Vessons.

After meeting Hazel at the local fair, new minister Edward Marston proposes to her. Having vowed to marry the first man who asks her, Hazel accepts. An infatuated Reddin begs that she marry him instead but she cannot break her word, and the wedding takes place. Reddin haunts Hazel until, guided by her mother's book of spells, she secretly meets him and returns to Undern as his mistress. Edward arrives to reclaim his bride and during the violent quarrel Reddin – himself a hunter – threatens to harm Foxy. Hazel is repulsed and returns with Edward.

When a delegation of church elders demand that he turn his unfaithful wife out, Edward decides to leave the church and start afresh. Meanwhile Hazel, hearing the local hunt in the adjoining fields, rescues Foxy but is herself pursued by the hounds. Reddin follows, trying to lift her out of the hounds' reach but Hazel refuses to drop the fox in the path of the dogs. Edward races to meet her as she approaches the house, but midway she and Foxy plunge to their deaths in an open, disused mineshaft as the call from the hunt leader echoes across the fields: 'Gone To Earth'.

Thanks to Shropshire, Miss Jones (especially), and the others, the film – though it lacks the touches for which Powell and Pressburger have made their name – is as pretty as those table

mats decorated with hunting scenes which one never wants oneself but which are fine for giving to other people as presents.
Daily Mail

Jennifer Jones... gives an appealing rendering of the role. Cyril Cusack is a very sincere parson.. Sybil Thorndike... David Farrar... Esmond Knight... George Cole, Edward Chapman and Hugh Griffith contribute to the starring cast. Never have I seen the English countryside in its many moods so beautifully photographed in discriminating Technicolor.
Picture Show

Primarily a simple yarn about simple people, it is without finesse, polish or sophistication. Dialog just about emerges from the monosyllabical state. Jones makes the character of Hazel Woodus a pathetic, winsome creature. It is a genuine and at times glowing performance.
Variety

THE ELUSIVE PIMPERNEL

(US: The Fighting Pimpernel)
(1950, 109 minutes) Technicolor. London Films. A Production of The Archers.
Written and Directed: Michael Powell and Emeric Pressburger, based on the novel by Baroness Orczy; *Presented by*: Alexander Korda;; *Director of Photography*: Christopher Challis; *Camera Operator*: Freddie Francis; *Film Editor*: Reginald Mills; *Process Shots*: W. Percy Day; *Technicolor Colour Director*: Natalie Kalmus; *Production Designer*: Hein Heckroth; *Assistant Designer:* Ivor Beddoes; *Art Director*: Arthur Lawson; *Location Art Director*: Joseph Bato; *Supervising Scenic Artist*: W.S. Robinson; *Music Score*: Brian Easdale, with the Philharmonia Orchestra; *Sound Recording*: Charles Poulton, Red Law; *Continuity*: Doreen North; *Hair Stylist*: Betty Cross; *Make-up*: Jimmy Vining; *Set Dresser*: Scott Slimon; *Assistant Producer*: George R. Busby; *Assistant Director*: Sydney Streeter
Cast: David Niven (Sir Percy Blakeney), Margaret Leighton (Marguerite Blakeney), Jack Hawkins (Prince of Wales), Cyril Cusack (Chauvelin), Robert Coote (Sir Andrew Ffoulkes), Arlette Marchal (Countesse de Tournai), Arthur Wontner (Lord Grenville), David Hutcheson (Lord Anthony Dewhurst), Charles Victor (Colonel Winterbottom), Eugene Deckers (Captain Merieres), Edmond Audran (Armand St Juste), Danielle Godet (Suzanne de Tournai), Gerard Nery (Philippe de Tournai), John Longden (Abbot), Richard George (Sir John Coke), David Oxley (Captain Duroc), Philip Stainton (Jellyband), Raymond Rollett (Bibot), Robert Griffiths (Trubshaw), George de Warfaz (Baron), Jane Gill Davies (Lady Grenville), John Fitzgerald (Sir Michael Travers), Terence Alexander (Duke of Dorset), Patrick MacNee (Hon John Bristow), Cherry Cottrell (Lady Bristow), Tommy Dugan (Earl of Sligo), John Fitchen (Nigel Seymour), John Hewitt (Major Pretty), Hugh Kelly (Mr Fitzdrummond), Richard Nairne (Beau Pepys)

In revolution-torn Paris of 1792, 'The Scarlet Pimpernel' rescues aristocrats from the guillotine and smuggles them to safety across the English Channel. Citizen Chauvelin determines that he will capture and unmask this folk hero and travels to England, suspecting the Pimpernel to be Sir Percy Blakeney. He forces Sir Percy's wife Marguerite to help him by threatening to expose her brother Armand.

Marguerite despises her husband as a worthless fop, while Percy for his part mistrusts Marguerite, believing she betrayed a French family to the government. Chauvelin learns the Pimpernel's identity and, realizing the truth herself, Marguerite races to Mont St Michel, the rendezvous of the Pimpernel and his men, only to be captured by the Chauvelin. Percy offers his own life in exchange for Marguerite's, but escapes the firing squad. As Chauvelin's men surround the castle they realize too late that the advancing high tide has cut off the Mont. The Pimpernel escapes by boat, he and Marguerite at last confident of each other's trust.

I must say without any beating about the bush that it is a sad let-down for the firm that produced the original 'Pimpernel' with Leslie Howard and considering the talents engaged in it, and the natural appeal of the subject, about as bad as it can be.
C.A. Lejeune, The Observer

The Elusive Pimpernel *has eluded Messrs Powell and Pressburger... [he] would need to have been played by a paragon combining the attributes of Chaplin and Valentino. One cannot blame David Niven for suggesting neither.*
Sunday Express

THE TALES OF HOFFMANN

(1951, 127 minutes; 115 minutes on general release) Technicolor. A Production of The Archers for London Films.

Written, Produced and Directed: Michael Powell and Emeric Pressburger; *Screenplay:* based on the opera by Jacques Offenbach; *Libretto:* Jules Barbier; *English translation:* Dennis Arundell; *Director of Photography:* Christopher Challis; *Camera Operator:* Freddie Francis; *Film Editor:* Reginald Mills; *Process Shots:* E. Hague; *Production Designer:* Hein Heckroth; *Art Director:* Arthur Lawson; *Assistant Designers:* Ivor Beddoes, Terence Morgan II; *Music:* Jacques Offenbach, conducted by Sir Thomas Beecham, with the Royal Philharmonic Orchestra; *Sound Recording:* Ted Drake, John Cox; *Choreography:* Frederick Ashton; *Choreography Assistants:* Alan Carter, Joan Harris; *Assistant Producer:* George R. Busby; *Assistant Director:* Sydney Streeter

Cast: Prologue and Epilogue: Robert Rounseville (Hoffmann), Pamela Brown (Nicklaus [sung by Monica Sinclair]), Robert Helpmann (Lindorf), Moira Shearer (Stella), Philp Leaver (Andreas), Meinhart Maur (Luther [sung by Fisher-Morgan]), Frederick Ashton (Kleinzack), Edmond Audran (Cancer)

The Tale of Olympia: Moira Shearer (Olympia [sung by Dorothy Bond]), Léonide Massine (Spalanzani [sung by Grahame Clifford]), Robert Helpmann (Coppelius [sung by Bruce Dargavel]), Robert Rounseville (Hoffmann), Frederick Ashton (Cochenille [sung by Murray Dickie])

The Tale of Giulietta: Ludmilla Tcherina (Giulietta [sung by Margherita Grandi]), Robert Helpmann (Dapertutto [sung by Bruce Dargavel]), Léonide Masssine (Schlemil [sung by Owen Brannigan]), Robert Rounseville (Hoffmann), Lionel Harris (Pitichinaccio [sung by Murray Dickie])

The Tale of Antonia: Ann Ayars (Antonia), Mogens Wieth (Crespel [sung by Owen Brannigan]), Robert Rounseville (Hoffmann), Léonide Massine (Franz [sung by Grahame Clifford]), Robert Helpmann (Dr Miracle [sung by Bruce Dargavel]), Antonia's mother (sung by Joan Alexander)

At the Nürnberg Opera House, E.T.A. Hoffmann, deeply in love with Stella, watches her perform the *Dragonfly* ballet. During the interval at Luther's Tavern, he tells the young students his 'three tales of my folly of love':

The Tale of Olympia: Hoffmann buys a pair of magic spectacles from puppet-makers Spalanzani and Coppelius which convince him that a full sized doll is a real woman. He falls in love with the woman Olympia but when Coppelius smashes the doll after falling out with Spalanzani, Hoffmann realizes he has been tricked.

The Tale of Giulietta: In Venice, courtesan Giulietta, under the power of Dapertutto, captures Hoffmann's reflection and with it his soul. A duel ends with Hoffmann killing Giulietta's former lover Schlemil. Finding that she has left with Dapertutto, Hoffmann smashes the mirror and is released.

The Tale of Antonia: Hoffmann falls in love with the seriously ill Antonia, who is forbiden to sing by her father Crespel. Told not to admit either Hoffmann or Dr Miracle, deaf servant Franz misunderstands and allows both to enter. Hoffmann makes Antonia promise not to sing, but Dr Miracle persuades her to disobey. After singing her song, she dies in Hoffmann's arms.

Epilogue: His tales over, Hoffmann falls into a drunken stupor. Stella appears and disappointedly looks down at him. Lindorf seizes the opportunity and together they exit, leaving Hoffmann alone to pursue his destiny as a poet.

The Tales of Hoffmann *is undoubtedly the most opulent, most expensive, most courageous and most exhausting effort yet made to bring opera to the screen… Sometimes the sensation is like hurtling through an art gallery in an express train with the steam whistle at full blast. Sometimes it is like sitting on a whirling roundabout sucking a peppermint stick.. Not for a single moment will* The Tales of Hoffmann *move you to laughter or tears.*
Milton Shulman, Evening Standard

The obvious care and effort that have gone into Hoffmann, the sometimes memorably contrived passages of virtuosity in the first half, make one reluctant to insist on the collapse of the work as a whole. Probably the material itself is quite intractable, but the trouble is that behind all the effects, the strivings, the opulence and the apparatus, there seems no clear sense of direction, no single purpose at all. In this way it is the most spectacular failure yet achieved by Powell and Pressburger, who seem increasingly to dissipate their gifts in a welter of aimless ingenuity.
Monthly Film Bulletin

OH, ROSALINDA!!

(1955, 101 minutes) Technicolor. Cinemascope. The Archers. A Michael Powell and Emeric Pressburger Presentation.
Written, Produced and Directed: Michael Powell and Emeric Pressburger; *Screenplay:* based on Johann Strauss' light opera *Die Fledermaus*; *New lyrics:* Dennis Arundell; *Director of Photography*: Christopher Challis; *Camera Operator:* Norman Warwick; *Film Editor:* Reginald Mills; *Production Designer*: Hein Heckroth; *Associate Art Director:* Arthur Lawson; *Assistant Designer:* Terence Morgan II; *Music:* Johann Strauss; *Music Director:* Fred Lewis; *Conductor:* Aleis Melichar with the Wiener Symphoniker Orchestra; *Sound Recording:* Leslie Hammond, Herbert Janeczka; *Production Manager:* Charles Orme; *Dubbing Editor:* Noreen Ackland; *Make-up:* Constance Reeve; *Hairdressing*: A.G. Scott; *Ludmilla Tcherina's clothes*: created by Jean Desses of Paris; *Associate Producer:* Sydney Streeter; *Assistant Director:* John Pellatt; *Choreography:* Alfred Rodriques
Cast: Anthony Quayle (General Orlofsky), Anton Walbrook (Dr Falke [sung by Walter Berry]), Richard Marner (Judge), Ludmilla Tcherina (Rosalinda [sung by Sari Barabas]), Michael Redgrave (Colonel Eisenstein), Mel Ferrer (Captain Alfred Westerman [sung by Alexander Young]), Nicholas Bruce (Hotel Receptionist), Anneliese Rothenberger (Adele), Dennis Price (Major Frank [sung by Dennis Dowling]), Oska Sima (Frosh)
The ladies: Barbara Archer, Betty Ash, Joyce Blair, Hildy Christian, Pamela Foster, Patricia Garnett, Annette Gibson, Eileen Gourley, Jean Grayston, Grizelda Hervey, Jill Ireland, Maya Koumain, Olga Lowe, Sara Luzita, Ingrid Marshall, Alicia Massy-Beresford, Eileen Sands, Herta Seydel, Anna Steele, Jennifer Walmsley, Dorothy Whitney, Prudence Hyman
The gentlemen: Michael Anthony, Igor Barczinsky, Cecil Bates, Richard Bennett, Nicholas Bruce, Ray Buckingham, Denis Carey, Rolf Carston, Terence Cooper, Robert Crewdston, Peter Darrell, Edward Forsyth, Roger Gage, David Gilbert, Robert Harrold, Jan Lawski, Raymond Lloyd, Richard Marner, William Martin, Kenneth Melville, Orest Orloff, Robert Ross, John Schlesinger, Frederick Schrecker, Maurice Metliss, Kenneth Smith

In Vienna, governed by Russia, Austria, Britain and Prussia, Dr Falke, known as 'The

Bat', is brought before the four-powered court after being made the victim of practical jokers Colonel Eisenstein and his wife Rosalinda. The authorities send for Eisenstein, who is confined to barracks for eight days.

As further revenge, Falke persuades Eisenstein to attend a masked ball without Rosalinda, who is visited by old flame Captain Alfred Westerman. Major Frank mistakes Westerman for Eisenstein and takes him into custody. Falke telephones Rosalinda and invites her to the ball where Eisenstein, not recognizing her, immediately begins to flirt with her. She leaves suddenly, taking with her Eisenstein's watch. At the barracks, Eisenstein finds Alfred in the cell intended for him, wearing his own dressing gown. He storms out to confront Rosalinda, followed by Alfred and Major Frank.

Falke and his guests eavesdrop as Eisenstein accuses his wife of being unfaithful with Alfred until Rosalinda produces the watch as proof of his own flirtatious ways. They realize that Falke has been behind the entire plot.

Oh, Rosalinda!! is a gay, lovely affair as maddening as that bewitching creature of whom the poet wrote: 'With all her faults I love her still'. It is a Powell and Pressburger picture, which inevitably means excellence and exasperation at the same time... [P & P] never did bother much about their audiences understanding what they were getting at. A pity, because in this film as always, they are shown as probably the most artistically enterprising of all our producers.
Jympson Marman, Evening News

A light and amusing idea... is here trampled under elephantine treatment... Three artists emerge with credit – Anton Walbrook (who is particularly clever in his delivery of the prologue to the film), Anneliese Rothenberger... and Anthony Quayle... while Michael Redgrave capers with, one feels, more goodwill than enjoyment.
Monthly Film Bulletin

THE SORCERER'S APPRENTICE

(1955, 30 minutes, later cut to 15 minutes) Technicolor. Cinemascope. Twentieth Century-Fox/Norddeutscher Rundfunk.
Director: Michael Powell; *Screenplay:* Dennis Arundell, based on a story by Goethe; *Photography:* Christopher Challis; *Camera Operator:* Freddie Francis; *Film Editor:* Reginald Mills; *Production Designer:* Hein Heckroth; *Choreography:* Helga Swedlund; *Music:* played by Hamburg State Opera Orchestra

THE BATTLE OF THE RIVER PLATE

(US: Pursuit of the Graf Spee)
(1956, 119 minutes; US: 106 minutes) Technicolor. VistaVision. Arcturus.
A Michael Powell and Emeric Pressburger Production.
Written, Produced and Directed: Michael Powell and Emeric Pressburger; *Director of Photography:* Christopher Challis; *Camera Operator:* Austin Dempster; *Film Editor:* Reginald Mills; *Production Designer:* Arthur Lawson; *Associate Art Director:* Donald Picton; *Artistic Adviser:* Hein Heckroth; *Music Score:* Brian Easdale; *Musical Director:* Frederick Lewis; *Sound Recordist:* C.C. Stevens, Gordon K. McCallum; *Assistant Producer:* Sydney Streeter; *Assistant Director:* Charles Orme; *Naval Adviser:* Captain F.S. Bell; *Technical Adviser:* Captain Patrick Dove
Cast: John Gregson (Captain Bell), Anthony Quayle (Commodore Harwood), Peter Finch (Captain Hans Langsdorff), Bernard Lee (Captain Patrick Dove), Ian Hunter (Captain Woodhouse), Jack Gwillim (Captain Parry), Anthony Bushell (Millington-Drake), Lionel Murton (Mike Fowler), Peter Illing (Dr Guani), Michael Goodliffe (Captain McCall), Patrick MacNee (Lt Cmdr Medley), Douglas Wilmer (M Desmoulins), William Squire (Ray Martin),

● **Michael Powell (beneath camera) directing operations during filming of** *The Battle of the River Plate* **aboard HMNZS** *Achilles*.

John Chandos (Dr Langmann), Andrew Cruickshank (Captain Stubs), Roger Delgado (Captain Varela), Christopher Lee (Manola), Edward Atienza (Pop), April Olrich (Dolores), over 100 other speaking parts (uncredited)
The following ships appeared in the film: HMS *Sheffield* (as HMS *Ajax*), INS *Delhi* (HMNZS *Achilles*), HMS *Jamaica* (HMS *Exeter*), US Heavy Cruiser *Salem* (*Admiral Graf Spee*) and HMS *Cumberland* (as herself)

In the first weeks of the Second World War, German crack pocket battleship *Admiral Graf Spee*, captained by Hans Langsdorff, inflicts heavy damage on British merchant shipping. Discovering the *Graf Spee*'s position, Commodore Harwood consults with Captains Bell of the *Exeter*, Woodhouse of *Ajax* and Parry of the New Zealand ship *Achilles*, gambling that the Germans will head for the River Plate before returning home.

A fierce battle rages throughout the following day, with *Exeter* suffering heavy damage. The *Graf Spee* escapes under cover of nightfall to neutral Montevideo harbour where, after frantic diplomatic negotiations, foreign minister Doctor Guani, acting under the Hague Convention, allows Langsdorff 72 hours to carry out such repairs as will make the vessel seaworthy without enhancing its fighting ability.

British Naval Intelligence meanwhile spread rumours of an advancing fleet awaiting the German ship as soon as it leaves port, although only the still damaged *Ajax* and *Achilles* are within striking distance. As the deadline approaches and the *Graf Spee* moves out of the harbour, the entire crew transfer to a German freighter as a series of explosions engulf their ship in flames. The British bluff has worked – Langsdorff has scuttled his vessel, believing escape impossible.

The Battle of the River Plate *is one of the better war films... I liked it as much for what it*

wasn't as for what it was. Heroic understatement has not been allowed to become a stylized obsession. The schoolboy pranksterism that mars many.. films has been avoided... The acting is scarcely more than formal participation – but Peter Finch manages in a few scenes to make a person out of Captain Langsdorff.
Time and Tide

Second thought on this film confirm my belief that it is one of the few British Royal Films that have really deserved the honour... Peter Finch's magnetic acting puts him in the forefront of British stars, and producers [Powell and Pressburger] have produced the battle sequences with a gun-roaring realism that almost jumps you out of your seat.
Roy Nash, Star

ILL MET BY MOONLIGHT

(US: Night Ambush)
(1956, 104 minutes; US: 93 minutes) VistaVision. Vega Productions. A Michael Powell and Emeric Pressburger Production.
Written, Produced and Directed: Michael Powell and Emeric Pressburger; *Screenplay*: based on the book by W. Stanley Moss; *Director of Photography:* Christopher Challis; *Camera Operator:* Austin Dempster; *Film Editor:* Arthur Stevens; *Special Effects:* Bill Warrington; *Art Director:* Alex Vetchinsky; *Music Score:* Mikis Theodorakis; *Music Director:* Frederic Lewis; *Sound Recordists:* Charles Knott, Gordon K. McCallum; *Sound Editor:* Archi Ludski; *Technical Advisers:* Micky Akoumianakis, Major Xan Flaiging; *Production Manager:* Jack Swinburne; *Dress Designer:* Nandi Routh; *Continuity:* Gladys Goldsmith; *Make-up:* Paul Rabiger; *Assistant Producer:* Sydney Streeter; *Assistant Director:* Charles Orme
Cast: Dirk Bogarde (Major Paddy Leigh-Fermor, also known as 'Philidem'), Marius Goring (General Karl Kreipe), David Oxley (Captain Billy Stanley Moss), Demitri Andreas (Niko), Cyril Cusack (Sandy), Laurence Payne (Manoli), Wolfe Morris (George), Michael Gough (Andoni Zoidakis), John Cairney (Elias), Brian Worth (Stratis Saviolkis), Rowland Bartrop (Micky Akoumianakis), George Egeniou (Charis Zographakis), Paul Stassino (Yami Katsias), Adeeb Assaly (Zahari), Theo Moreas (Village Priest), Takis Frangofinos (Michali), Christopher Lee, Peter Augustine, John and Phyllia Houseman, David McCallum

On occupied Crete British Major Paddy Leigh-Fermor plans to demoralize the German forces by kidnapping Commander in Chief General Kreipe with the help of Captain William Stanley Moss and the local underground resistance movement.

Disguised as German Military Police, they hijack Kreipe's car and, concealed by a heavy mist, thread their way on foot across the mountains unseen. Kreipe attempts to delay escape by claiming to have injured a shoulder, and sets a trail for his men to follow using his hat, medals and buttons.

The kidnappers find the rendezvous point surrounded by Germans, but after Kreipe has tried to bribe one of the Cretan boys, his plan backfires and the troops leave the spot unprotected. On the beach, Leigh-Fermor and Moss realize that they do not know how to signal morse to the waiting British ship. Kreipe admonishes them as amateurs until Sandy, a British officer masquerading as a Cretan, signals to the vessel and they are picked up. Once aboard ship, Kreipe is handed his hat, medals and buttons, collected by Moss during the escape, and realizes that his captors are not such amateurs as he believed.

The film was ostensibly filmed somewhere on location in the Mediterranean. Some of the rocky paths and stones, however, have the sort of quality more usually associated with studios

specialising in photographs of 'Baby's first trip to the seaside'.
Daily Worker

One waits in vain for some of the physical excitement which was communicated in W. Stanley Moss's book; but the Powell and Pressburger team show little confidence in the potentialities of the battle of wits between the kidnappers and their distinguished quarry. The flight across the mountains seems uneventful, so that attention is too easily distracted – pleasantly by the attractive locations, but rather too obviously by the patriotic music score of Mikis Theodorakis... Dirk Bogarde's polite and restrained 'heroic' style is here somewhat over-indulged.
Monthly Film Bulletin

LUNA DE MIEL

(Honeymoon)
(1959, 109 minutes, UK release version: 90 minutes) Technicolor. Technirama.
Everdene. A Michael Powell production for Suevia Films-Cesário Gonsález (Spain).
Director: Michael Powell; *Producers:* Cesário Gonsález and Michael Powell; *Screenplay:* Michael Powell, Luis Escobar; *Director of Photography:* Georges Périnal; *Associate Photography:* Gerry Turpin; *Film Editors:* Peter Taylor, John V. Smith; *Art Direction and Costumes:* Ivor Beddoes; *Assistant Art Directors:* Eduardo Torre la Fuente, Roberto Carpio, Judy Jordan; *Music Score:* Mikis Theodorakis; *Sound Recordists:* John Cox, Fernando Bernáldes, Janet Davidson; *Production Supervisor:* Jaime Prades; *Associate Producers:* Sydney Streeter, Judith Coxhead, William J. Paton; *Associate Director:* Ricardo Blasco
Ballets: El Amor Brujo: *Music:* Manuel de Falla; *Sets:* Rafael Durancamps; *Choreography:* Antonio; *Soloist:* Maria Clara Alcala; *Guest dancer:* Léonide Massine; *Screenplay:* Gregorio Martinez Sierra
Los Amantes de Teruel: *Music:* Mikis Theodorakis, conducted by Sir Thomas Beecham; *Choreography:* Léonide Massine
Cast: Anthony Steel (Kit Kelly), Ludmilla Tcherina (Anna Kelly), Antonio (Himself), Rosita Segovia (Rosita), Léonide Massine ('Der Geist'), Juan Carmona (Pepe Niete), Carmen Rojas (Lucia), Maria Gamez, Diego Hurtado and Antonio's Spanish Ballet Troupe

Honeymooning in Spain with his bride Anna, Australian farmer Kit Kelly offers a lift to a stranded motorist who they discover is a famous dancer. Learning that Anna is a former ballerina, Antonio asks her to join his company, but the newlyweds insist on continuing with their journey. Antonio meets them at every stop and persists with his efforts to persuade her to dance with him. Kit becomes increasingly jealous, more so when he finds Anna rehearsing with Antonio. Anna later dreams of dancing in Antonio's ballet, but – 'sleep-dancing' out to the edge of the roof of the hotel – is rescued by Kit before the dance reaches its tragic conclusion. They leave Madrid to continue their honeymoon. Antonio announces that his dance company is about to embark on their own world tour. He will be looking for Anna as they travel.

Basically the film is an enormous travel poster of the most blatant kind, full of fast cars, sump-tuous hotels, elegant dresses, flowing money and lovely scenery with never a spot of dirt or a hint of discontent to cloud its beautiful vision. But even Georges Périnal's delicately coloured landscapes cannot disguise the thinness of the story or the feeble acting... it confirms the recent decline of its director.
Monthly Film Bulletin

PEEPING TOM

(1960, 109 minutes, US: 86 minutes) Eastman Colour. A Michael Powell Production for Michael Powell (Theatre) Ltd.

Produced and Directed: Michael Powell; *Original Story and Screenplay:* Leo Marks; *Director of Photography:* Otto Heller; *Camera Operator:* Gerry Turpin; *Film Editor:* Noreen Ackland; *Art Director:* Arthur Lawson; *Assistant Art Director:* Ivor Beddoes; *Music Score:* Brian Easdale; *Percussion Number:* Wally Scott; *Dance Music:* Freddie Phillips; *Solo Piano:* Gordon Watson; *Sound Recording:* C.C. Stevens, Gordon K. McCallum; *Sound Editor:* Malcolm Cooke; *Anna Massey's dresses:* Polly Peck; *Moira Shearer's costumes:* John Tullis of Horrockses; *Hats:* Millinery Guild; *Make-up:* W.J. Partleton; *Wardrobe:* Dickie Richardson; *Continuity:* Rita Davison; *Assistant Director:* Ted Sturgio; *Assistant Producer:* Albert Fennell

Cast: Carl Boehm (Mark Lewis), Moira Shearer (Vivian), Anna Massey (Helen Stephens), Maxine Audley (Mrs Stephens), Brenda Bruce (Dora), Esmond Knight (Arthur Baden), Martin Miller (Dr Rosan), Michael Goodliffe (Don Jarvis), Jack Watson (Inspector Gregg), Shirley Anne Field (Diane Ashley), Pamela Green (Milly), Nigel Davenport (Sergeant Miller), Miles Malleson (Elderly Gentleman), Bartlett Mullins (Mr Peters), Brian Wallace (Tony), Susan Travers (Lorraine), Maurice Durant (Publicity Chief), Brian Worth (Assistant Director), Veronica Hurst (Miss Simpson), Alan Rolfe (Store Detective), John Dunbar (Police Doctor), Guy Kingsley-Poynter (Cameraman), Keith Baxter (Baxter), Peggy Thorpe-Bates (Mrs Partridge), John Barrard (Small Man), Roland Curram (Extra), John Chappell (Clapper Boy), Michael Powell (Professor A.N. Lewis), Columba Powell (Mark as a child)

Following the murder of a prostitute Mark Lewis films onlookers' faces from across the street. Helen Stephens and her blind mother live in the flat below Mark and Mrs Stephens senses something odd about the boy. Mark shows Helen film of himself as a child with his father, a scientist studying the psychology of fear. Helen is appalled at the film, which shows the child's terrified reactions to his father's experiments.

Later, at the deserted film studios where Mark works, he pretends to make a screen test of Vivian but instead films her murder and hides the body, recording the horrified reactions to its discovery the next day during rehearsals. Learning that Mark is the son of the famous Professor Lewis, Inspector Gregg has him followed. That night, Milly is murdered at the studio where Mark photographs models for 'art' magazines and the police head for his home where Helen has just discovered the film of Vivian's murder.

Mark tells Helen how he kills his victims, using the sharpened leg of his camera tripod while focusing a mirror on their faces so that they can see their own fear. Realizing he cannot escape, Mark secures his camera to the wall to film his own suicide. The police discover him dead, stabbed like the others – the room filled with the long ago tape-recorded sound of his father telling him not to be frightened.

Mr Michael Powell, who produces with the finesse one expects of him, works all this up into a sufficiently nasty climax... Mr. Powell is a director who knows where he is going; if he makes a thriller, it will thrill. That this does so only intermittently is due to a clinical interest in the hero's psychopathy... The acting does its best to supply the missing tension... Mr Boehm sees the subtleties of his part and plays well, creating a good deal of sympathy by his realization that he cannot escape from his mania.
The Times

The only satisfactory way to dispose of Peeping Tom *would be to shovel it up and flush it swiftly down the nearest sewer. Even then the stench would remain.. It is no surprise that this is the work of Michael Powell, who displayed his vulgarity in such films as* A Matter of Life and Death*,*

● The end of *Peeping Tom* – Mark (Carl Boehm) shoots the ultimate home movie – his own suicide.

The Red Shoes *and* Tales of Hoffmann, *and the bizarre tendencies of his curious mind in* A Canterbury Tale *where the story consisted of Eric Portman pouring glue onto girls' hair. In* Peeping Tom *his self-exposure goes even further. He not only plays the sadistic father, but uses his own child as the victim...The immediate answer to trash like* Peeping Tom *is not more censorship, for that could only worsen a position rapidly growing impossible. The box-office is the real test – and not the West End box-office where anything that causes a stir in the press stands a chance of attracting a queue, but the provincial and suburban box-office. And that's where you come in – or rather, I hope, where you don't.*
Derek Hill, Tribune

The director is Michael Powell (of Red Shoes *fame), and he has made the film with some distinctive touches of technical brilliance. Why he has made it, however, I do not know. As a thriller it fails to thrill. As a shocker it succeeds only in being nauseating for the sake of nausea. This is a sick film – sick and nasty.*
Derek Monsey, Daily Express

Powell has directed with imagination, but he might well have tightened up the story line. The standout feature is some fascinating photography by Otto Heller [who] does much to give Peeping Tom *a veneer which the story does not entirely deserve.*
Variety

THE QUEEN'S GUARDS

(1961, 110 minutes) Technicolor. Imperial. A Michael Powell Production.
Produced and Directed: Michael Powell; *Screenplay:* Roger Milner, from an idea by Simon Harcourt-Williams; *Director of Photography:* Gerry Turpin; *Camera Operators:* Derek Browne, Austin Dempster, Skeets Kelly, Robert Walker, James Bawden, Robert Huke, Dudley Lovell,

Norman Warwick; *Film Editor:* Noreen Ackland; *Art Director:* Wilfred Shingleton; *Music Score:* Brian Easdale; *Sound Recording:* James Shields, Red Law; *Costumes:* Bridget Sellers; *Assistant Director:* Sydney Streeter; *Production Manager:* John Wilcox; *Associate Producer:* Simon Harcourt-Williams; *Military Music:* played by the Mounted Band of The Horse Guards and The Massed Bands Drum and Pipes of the Brigade of Guards

Cast: Daniel Massey (John Fellowes), Raymond Massey (Captain Fellowes), Robert Stephens (Henry Wynne-Walton), Peter Myers (Gordon Davidson), Ursula Jeans (Mrs Fellowes), Judith Stott (Ruth), Frank Lawton (Commander Hewson), Anthony Bushell (Major Cole), Ian Hunter (Dobbie), Jess Conrad (Dankworth), Duncan Lamont (Major Wilkes), Elizabeth Shepherd (Susan), Patrick Connor (Brewer), Jack Allen (Brigadier Cummings), Andrew Crawford (Biggs), Jack Watson (Sgt Johnson), Nigel Green (Abu Sidbar), Jack Watling (Captain Shergold), William Young (Williams), Eileen Peel (Mrs Wynne-Walton), Laurence Payne (Farinda), William Fox (Mr Walters), Roland Curram (Kenyon), Anthony Selby (Kishu), Cornel Lucas (Photographer), John Chappell (Private Walsh), René Cutforth (Commentator)

Captains John Fellowes and Henry Wynne-Walton pass through their training at Sandhurst and are sent to the Middle East; John to lead a paratroop regiment while Henry commands a platoon of armoured cars of the Household Brigade.

John's father, a disabled ex-Guards officer, constantly compares him to his elder brother David, killed in the desert during the war, while his mother still hopes that David is alive and will one day return. Discovering the truth about his brother's death, John determines during his own desert campaign to match his brother's courage and actions.

As the Trooping the Colour ceremony takes place, with John leading the Escort and Henry leading the Sovereign's Escort, Captain Fellowes watches the parade, finally proud of his second son.

I can't imagine anyone who will fail to be thrilled by this picture. Yet Michael Powell... tells me that huge chunks were cut out and that a three hour film has been slashed to 1 hour 50 minutes. That is a crime against a great subject and the work of one of our best directors. Why can't Wardour Street recognise an epic when they see one ?
The People

This flag-waving museum piece would be distressing if it weren't so inept... [the actors] battle manfully with dialogue and characters as dated as a Crimean cavalry charge. The film could scarcely be taken as a tribute to the Guards except, just possibly, by elderly aunts in Cheltenham.
Monthly Film Bulletin

BLUEBEARD'S CASTLE
(1964, 60 minutes) Technicolor. Norman Foster Productions/Süddeutscher Rundfunk. *Director:* Michael Powell; *Producer:* Norman Foster; *Screenplay* based on Bela Bartok's opera Bluebeard's Castle with libretto by Bela Balazs; *Conducted:* Milan Horvath; *Photography:* Hannes Staudinger; *Film Editor:* Paula Dvorak; *Production Designer:* Hein Heckroth; *Art Director:* Gerd Krauss
Cast: Norman Foster (Bluebeard), Anna Raquel Sartre (Judit)

THEY'RE A WEIRD MOB
(1966, 112 minutes) Eastman Colour. Williamson-Powell. A Michael Powell Production.
Directed and Produced: Michael Powell; *Screenplay:* Richard Imrie, from the novel by John O'Grady; *Director of Photography:* Arthur Grant; *Camera Operators:* Keith Loone, Graham Lind,

Dennis Hill; *Film Editor*: G. Turney-Smith; *Art Director*: Dennis Gentle; *Music Score:* Lawrence Leonard, Alan Boustead; *Songs*: 'Big Country' and 'In This Man's Country' by Reen Devereaux; 'I Kiss You, You Kiss Me" by Walter Chiari; 'Cretan Dance' by Mikis Theodorakis; *Musical Director*: Leonard Lawrence; *Sound Recordist*: Alan Allen; *Dubbing*: Ted Karnon; *Sound Editors*: Don Saunders, Bill Creed; *Dress Designer*: Chris Jacovides; *Wardrobe Mistress*: Barbara Turnbull; *Make-up:* Joan Adelsteine, Barbara Still; *Hairdresser*: Leon d'Auinals; *Set Dresser*: David Copping; *Technical Adviser:* John O'Grady; *Dialogue Coach*: Max Meldrum; *Casting:* Gloria Payten; *Production Supervisor:* Lee Robinson; *Location Manager*: Jefferson Jackson; *Unit Manager*: Bruce Bennett; *Continuity*: Doreen Soan; *Associate Producer*: John Pellatt; *Assistant Director*: Claude Watson
Cast: Walter Chiari (Nino Culotta), Clare Dunne (Kay Kelly), Chips Rafferty (Harry Kelly), Alida Chelli (Guiliana), Ed Devereaux (Joe), Slim de Grey (Pat), John Meillon (Dennis), Charles Little (Jimmy), Anne Haddy (Barmaid), Jack Allen (Fat man in bar), Red Moore (Texture man), Ray Hatley (Newsboy), Tony Bonner (Lifesaver), Alan Lander (Charlie), Keith Petersen (Drunk man on ferry), Muriel Steinbeck (Mrs Kelly), Gloria Dawn (Mrs Chapman), Jeanne Dryman (Betty), Gita Rivera (Maria), Judith Arthy (Dixie), Doreen Warburton (Edie)

Arriving in Australia to work on his cousin Leonardo's newspaper, Italian-born Nino Culotta finds that Leonardo has fled to Canada, leaving a string of debts behind him. Kay Kelly is one of those owed money and she tells Nino bluntly that she does not approve of 'dagos'. Nino finds work as a builder's labourer, and begins to repay Kay what is owed to her. When she is later advised by her solicitor not to accept any more money from him she attempts to return it, causing further disagreement. After sleeping rough in the deserted newspaper offices, Nino moves in with workmate Joe and his family. Meeting at an Italian restaurant, Nino and Kay realize that they have fallen in love. Her father Harry however, insists that he has no time for 'dagos', but eventually softens toward Nino, who – after a year in Australia – is now one of the 'mob'.

The week's best film. It is a simple and heart-warming picture, directed with generous understanding by the talented Michael Powell.
Sunday Express

The oddest thing about this dreadful film is that one cannot walk out on it. In spite of the ghastly material – and this is no exaggeration – Mr Powell continues to exert a fascination that few British directors can equal.
The Guardian

For the first half, the film strives too hard to be funny and concentrates too much upon the strange Aussie lingo. Once it setles down to telling a story... it is stronger entertainment.
Variety

SEBASTIAN

(US: Mister Sebastian)
(1967, 100 minutes) Eastman Colour. Maccius.
Director: David Greene; *Producers*: Herbert Brodkin and Michael Powell; *Screenplay:* Gerald Vaughan-Hughes, based on an original story by Leo Marks; *Director of Photography*: Gerald Fisher; *Film Editor*: Brian Smedley-Aston; *Production Designer*: Wilfred Shingleton; *Art Director*: Fred Carter; *Set Decorator*: Terence Morgan II; *Music Score*: Jerry Goldsmith; *Song:* 'Here Comes The Night' by Jerry Goldsmith and Hal Shafer, sung by Anita Harris; *Sound Recording*: H.L. Bird, Gerry Humphreys; *Production Manager:* Clifton Brandon; *Associate Producer:* John Pellatt; *Assistant Director*: Gordon Gilbert
Cast: Dirk Bogarde (Sebastian), Susannah York (Becky Howard), Lilli Palmer (Elsa Shahn), John Gielgud (Head of Intelligence), Janet Munro (Carol), Margaret Johnson (Miss Elliott), Nigel

Davenport (General Phillips), Ronald Fraser (Toby), John Ronane (Jameson), Susan Whitman (Tilly), Ann Beach (Pamela), Ann Sidney (Naomi), Veronica Clifford (Ginny), Jeanne Roland (Randy), Lyn Pinkney (Joan), Louise Pernell (Thelma), Donald Sutherland (Ackerman), Alan Freeman (TV Disc Jockey), Charles Lloyd Pack (Chess player), Hayward Morse, Portland Mason, James Belchamber, Charles Farrell

Oxford professor Sebastian offers Becky Howard a job in his Secret Service code-breaking department, but when Elsa Shahn leaks information to a left-wing organization he is forced to resign. The Head of Intelligence asks Sebastian's help in breaking a new code used by Russian satellites. Becky has meanwhile left the department and Sebastian finally locates her, discovering that she has a child – his son. Playing with the infant, the sound of the baby's rattle suddenly gives him a vital clue to the new code.

Greene's direction is undercut by a script which toys with an interesting idea and then abandons it for a string of anti-heroic platitudes and a scrappily engineered conclusion... Nevertheless, David Greene has an eye for detail which makes the film always attractive to look at.. and he gets a solidly intelligent performance from Bogarde and spirited support from Susannah York.
Monthly Film Bulletin

AGE OF CONSENT

(1969, 103 minutes, UK: 98 minutes) Eastman Colour. Nautilus Productions.
Director: Michael Powell; *Producers*: James Mason and Michael Powell;
Screenplay: Peter Yeldham, based on the novel by Norman Lindsay; *Director of Photography*: Hannes Staudinger; *Underwater Photography*: Ron Taylor; *Film Editor*: Anthony Buckley; *Art Director*: Dennis Gentle; *Set Decorator*: Bill Piggott; *Music Score*: Stanley Myers; *Sound Editor*: Tim Wellburn; *Sound Recordist*: Paul Ennis, Lloyd Colman; *Animal Handler*: Scotty Denholm; *Associate Producer*: Michael Pate; *Assistant Director*: David Crocker; *Production Supervisor*: Brian Chirlian; *Production Manager*: Kevin Powell
Cast: James Mason (Bradley Morahan), Helen Mirren (Cora), Jack MacGowran (Nat Kelly), Neva Carr-Glyn (Ma Ryan), Antonia Katsaros (Isabel Marley), Michael Boddy (Hendricks), Harold Hopkins (Ted Farrell), Slim de Grey (Cooley), Max Meldrum (TV interviewer), Frank Thring (Godfrey), Dora Hing (Receptionist), Clarissa Kaye (Meg), Judy McGrath (Grace), Lenore Katon (Edna), Diane Strachan (Susie), Roberta Grant (Ivy), Prince Nial (Jasper), Hudson Fausset (New Yorker), Peggy Cass (New Yorker's wife), Eric Reiman (Art lover), Tommy Hanlon Jnr (Levi-Strauss), Geoff Cartwright (Newsboy)

Disillusioned artist Brad Morahan escapes New York for his Australian homeland seeking solitude but instead discovers alcoholic Ma Ryan and her granddaughter Cora, who sits as his model. A visit from old acquaintance Nat Kelly ends with Kelly stealing $300 from Brad before leaving the island in a stolen boat. Ma discovers Brad has been sketching her granddaughter and in an argument with Cora, the old woman falls from a cliff and is killed. The police investigation finds that the fall was an accident, and Cora offers Brad her money to make up for that stolen by Kelly. Brad refuses, realizing that the girl has restored meaning to his work and life. When Kelly is apprehended and the money returned, Brad and Cora are left to themselves at last.

I tremendously admire James Mason and believed, until I saw Age of Consent, *that he could do no wrong... It is best forgiven and forgotten.*
Penelope Mortimer, Observer

Michael Powell's film at least maintains his long-standing reputation as an original, among its

sophisticated (or Lawrentian) native daydream with cracking bursts of romping and raucousness.
Penelope Houston, Spectator

The film has plenty of corn, is sometimes too slow, repetitive and badly edited...Yet [it] has
immense charm, and the photography and superb scenery make it a good travelog ad for the Great
Barrier Reef.
Variety

THE BOY WHO TURNED YELLOW

(1972, 55 minutes) Eastman Colour. Roger Cherrill. Children's Film Foundation.
Director: Michael Powell; *Screenplay:* Emeric Pressburger from his original story *The Wife of Father*
Christmas; Director of Photography: Christopher Challis; *Film Editor:* Peter Boita; *Art Director:*
Bernard Sarron; *Electronic Music Score:* Patrick Gowers, David Vorhaus; *Sound Editor:* Roger
Harrison; *Sound Recording:* Bob Jones, Ken Barber; *Production Manager:* Gus Angus; *Assistant*
Director: Neil Vine-Miller; *Assistant Producer:* Drummond Challis
Cast: Mark Dightam (John Saunders), Robert Eddison (Nick), Helen Weir (Mrs Saunders), Brian
Worth (Mr Saunders), Esmond Knight (Doctor), Laurence Carter (Schoolteacher), Patrick
McAlinney (Supreme Beefeater), Lem Kitaj (Munro)

Sent home from school after falling asleep during a lesson on electricity, John is suddenly turned yellow, as are his fellow passengers on the Underground. A doctor confirms that there is nothing seriously wrong, and a later television discussion concludes
that the cause is 'something from outer space'.

  During the night, a voice from the television wakes John who switches on the set.
'Nick' – short for 'Electronic' – appears in the room and takes John travelling on electrical waves to the Tower of London where they recover John's pet mouse Alice, but
John is arrested and charged with treason. He is found guilty and sentenced to be executed, but asks to be allowed to watch television as a last request and escapes on the
electrical waves, returning home his normal colour again.

The Powell-Pressburger team returns after a fifteen-year absence in a film that slips rather disap-
pointingly from its initial promise...The brief of a 'children's film' seems in this case to have been
an insuperable restriction.. for all the sumptuousness of the colour effects, it seems unlikely that
children will be satisfied with so little in the way of explanation, or with the cursory excitement
of the escapade in the Tower.
Monthly Film Bulletin

RETURN TO THE EDGE OF THE WORLD

(1978, 85 minutes) Poseidon Films. Presented by Frixos Constantine and Michael
Powell.
Director: Michael Powell; *Producers:* Michael Powell and Sydney Streeter; *Screenplay:* Michael
Powell; *Photography:* Brian Mitchison; *Film Editor:* Peter Mayhew; *Music Score:* Brian Easdale;
Sound: David Hahn

PAVLOVA – A WOMAN FOR ALL TIME

(1983) Mosfilm/Poseidon Productions.
Director: Emil Lotianou; *Supervisor* (English language version): Michael Powell
Cast: Galina Baliaeva, James Fox, Sergei Shakourov, Vsevolod Larionov, Lina Boultakova, Georgio
Dimitriou, Martin Scorsese, Bruce Forsyth, Roy Kinnear

TV work

ESPIONAGE: Never Turn Your Back on a Friend
(1963, 48 minutes) ATV/NBC/Plautus (UK television).

Director: Michael Powell; *Producer*: George Justin; *Executive Producer*: Herbert Hirschman; *Associate Producer*: John Pellatt; *Assistant Director*: Bruce Sherman; *Screenplay*: Mel Davenport; *Photography*: Ken Hodges; *Camera Operator*: Herbert Smith; *Film Editor*: John Victor-Smith; *Production Designer*: Wilfred Shingleton; *Art Director*: Tony Woollard; *Music Score*: Malcolm Arnold; *Sound Recording*: David Bowen; *Sound Editor*: Dennis Rogers

Cast: George Voskovec (Professor Kuhn), Donald Madden (Anaconda), Mark Eden (Wicket), Julian Glover (Tovarich), Pamela Brown (Miss Jensen)

ESPIONAGE: A Free Agent
(1964, 48 minutes) ATV/NBC/Plautus (UK television).

Director: Michael Powell; *Producer*: George Justin; *Executive Producer*: Herbert Hirschman; *Associate Producer*: John Pellatt; *Assistant Director*: Jake Wright; *Screenplay*: Leo Marks; *Photography*: Geoffrey Faithfull; Camera Operator: Alan McCabe; *Film Editor*: John Victor-Smith; *Production Designer*: Wilfred Shingleton; *Art Director*: Anthony Woollard; *Music Score*: Benjamin Frankel; *Sound Recording*: Cyril Smith; *Sound Editor*: Dennis Rogers

Cast: Anthony Quayle (Philip), Sian Phillips (Anna), Norman Foster (Max), George Mikell (Peter), John Wood (Douglas), John Abineri (Town Clerk), Ernst Waldner (Watch Factory Mechanic), Gertan Klauber (Innkeeper), Vivienne Drummond (Miss Weiss), Jan Conrad (Chief Mechanic)

THE DEFENDERS: The Sworn Twelve
(1965, 50 minutes) CBS/Plautus (US television).

Director: Michael Powell; *Producer*: Herbert Brodkin; *Screenplay*: Edward DeBlasio

Cast: E.G. Marshall, Robert Reed, Murray Hamilton, King Donovan, Ruby Dee, Jerry Orbach

THE NURSES: A39846
(1965, 50 minutes) CBS/Plautus (US television).

Director: Michael Powell; *Producer*: Herbert Brodkin; *Screenplay*: George Bellak

Cast: Michael Tolan, Shirl Conway, Joseph Campanella, Jean-Pierre Aumont, Kermit Murdock

Selective bibliography

Christie, Ian, *Arrows of Desire,* Waterstone, 1985

Clark, Kenneth, *The Other Half,* John Murray, 1977

Farrar, David, *No Royal Road,* Mortimer Publications, 1947

Faulkner, Trader, *Peter Finch, A Biography,* Angus & Robertson, 1979

Godden, Rumer, *A House with Four Rooms,* Macmillan, 1989

Mason, James, *Before I Forget,* Hamish Hamilton, 1981

McCallum, John, *Life with Googie,* Heinemann, 1979

Powell, Michael, *A Life in Movies,* Heinemann, 1985

Powell, Michael, *Edge of the World,* Faber and Faber, 1990

Powell, Michael, *Million Dollar Movie,* Heinemann, 1992

Robson, E.W. and M.M., *The Shame and Disgrace of Colonel Blimp – The True Story behind the Film,* The Sidneyan Society, 1944

Badder, David, 'Powell and Pressburger: The War Years', *Sight and Sound,* Winter 1978/79

Cardiff, Jack, *The Times,* 23 February 1990

Cook, Pam, 'Gone to Earth', *Monthly Film Bulletin,* 53, 1986

Christie, Ian, 'Powell & Pressburger: putting back the pieces', *Monthly Film Bulletin,* December 1984

Gough-Yates, Kevin, 'Interviews with Michael Powell and Emeric Pressburger, September, November 1970', NFT 1971

The Guardian, 'Interview with Michael Powell', 7 May 1975

The Independent, 'Michael Powell's Ondine', 29 April 1989

The Observer, 'Interview with Michael Powell', 26 June 1988

O'Grady, John, 'Filming the Weird Mob', *The Bulletin,* 22 January 1966

Powell, Michael, 'A Matter of Life', *The Observer,* 14 February 1988

Powell, Michael, 'Mr Powell Replies', *Picturegoer,* 30 December 1950

Sharp, Rhoderick, Michael Powell's 60 Glorious Years', *Glasgow Herald,* 9 April 1985

The Times, 'Mr Michael Powell on making Horror Films', 5 July 1960

Williams, Tony, 'Interview with Michael Powell', *Films and Filming,* November 1981

Appendix A

Awards

Although one of the most successful and respected of British directors, Michael Powell failed to receive a single mention in that category at the annual American 'Oscars', although he did receive a nomination as co-screenwriter (with Emeric Pressburger) of *One of Our Aircraft is Missing*. Prior to 1960, the only British directors to win Academy Awards had been Frank Lloyd in 1933 (*Cavalcade*) and David Lean (*Bridge over the River Kwai*, 1957). Nevertheless, Powell and Pressburger were responsible for some of the most honoured British movies produced between 1940 and 1960.

The Thief of Bagdad
Academy Awards: Colour Cinematography (Georges Périnal); Colour Art Direction (W. Percy Day; William Cameron Menzies; Frederick Pusey; Ferdinand Bellan); Special Effects (Lawrence Butler). *Nomination*: Musical Score (Miklos Rozsa)

49th Parallel
Academy Award: Best Original Story (Emeric Pressburger)

One of Our Aircraft is Missing
Academy Award Nominations: Best Screenplay (Emeric Pressburger; Michael Powell); Special Effects (Ronald Neame; C.C. Stevens)

Black Narcissus
Academy Awards: Colour Cinematography (Jack Cardiff); Art Direction (Alfred Junge); Set Decoration (Alfred Junge)

The Red Shoes
Academy Awards: Musical Score (Brian Easdale); Colour Art Direction (Hein Heckroth); Set Decoration (Arthur Lawson)

The Tales of Hoffmann
Academy Award Nominations: Art Direction; Set Decoration; Costume Design (Hein Heckroth). Special Jury Prize; Prize of Commission Superieure Technique; Cannes Festival

Honeymoon
Special Prize of Commission Supérieure Technique; Cannes Festival

The Boy Who Turned Yellow
Children's Film Foundation Award

Powell received several personal awards including the Fellowship of the British Film Institute, the 'Rosebud' (an American award voted for by directors and named in honour of Orson Welles) and the Life Achievement Award at the Cannes Festival.

Appendix B

The films of Emeric Pressburger

ABSCHIED (Farewell)
(1930) UFA, Germany.
Director: Robert Siodmak; *Screenplay*: Emeric Pressburger and Irma Von Cube

DANN SCHON LIEBRE LEBERTRAN (I'd Rather Have Cod Liver Oil)
(1930) UFA, Germany.
Director: Max Ophuls; *Screenplay*: Emeric Pressburger, Erich Kastner and Max Ophuls, based on Kastner's story

DAS EKEL (The Scoundrel)
(1931) UFA, Germany.
Directors: Franz Wenzler and Eugen Schüfftan. *Screenplay*: Emeric Pressburger, from an idea by Reimann and Impekoven

DER KLEINE SEITENSPRUNG (The Little Escapade)
(1931) UFA, Germany.
Director: Reinhold Schünzel; *Screenplay*: Emeric Pressburger and Reinhold Schünzel, from an idea by Schünzel (French version *Le Petit Ecart* directed by Schünzel and Henri Chomette)

RONNY
(1931) UFA, Germany.
Director: Reinhold Schünzel; *Screenplay*: Pressburger and Schünzel (French version directed by Roger Le Bon)

DAS SCHONE ABENTEUR (The Happy Adventure)
(1932) UFA, Germany.
Director: Reinhold Schünzel; *Screenplay*: Emeric Pressburger and Reinhold Schünzel, based on a play by Robert de Fiers, Gaston Armand de Caillavet and Etienne Rey (French version *La Belle Aventure* directed by Roger Le Bon)

SEHNSUCHT (Yearning 202)
(1932) Deutsch-Osterreichische, Germany/Austria.
Director: Max Neufeld; *Screenplay*: Emeric Pressburger, Irmgard Von Cube and Karl Farkas (French version *Désir 22* or *Une Jeune Fille et un Million* directed by Fred Ellis)

UND ES LEUCHTET DIE PUSSTA (And the Plains are Gleaming)
(1933) UFA/Hunnia Film, Germany, Budapest.
Director: Heinz Hille; *Screenplay*: Emeric Pressburger based on novel *The Old Crook* by Koloman Mikszath

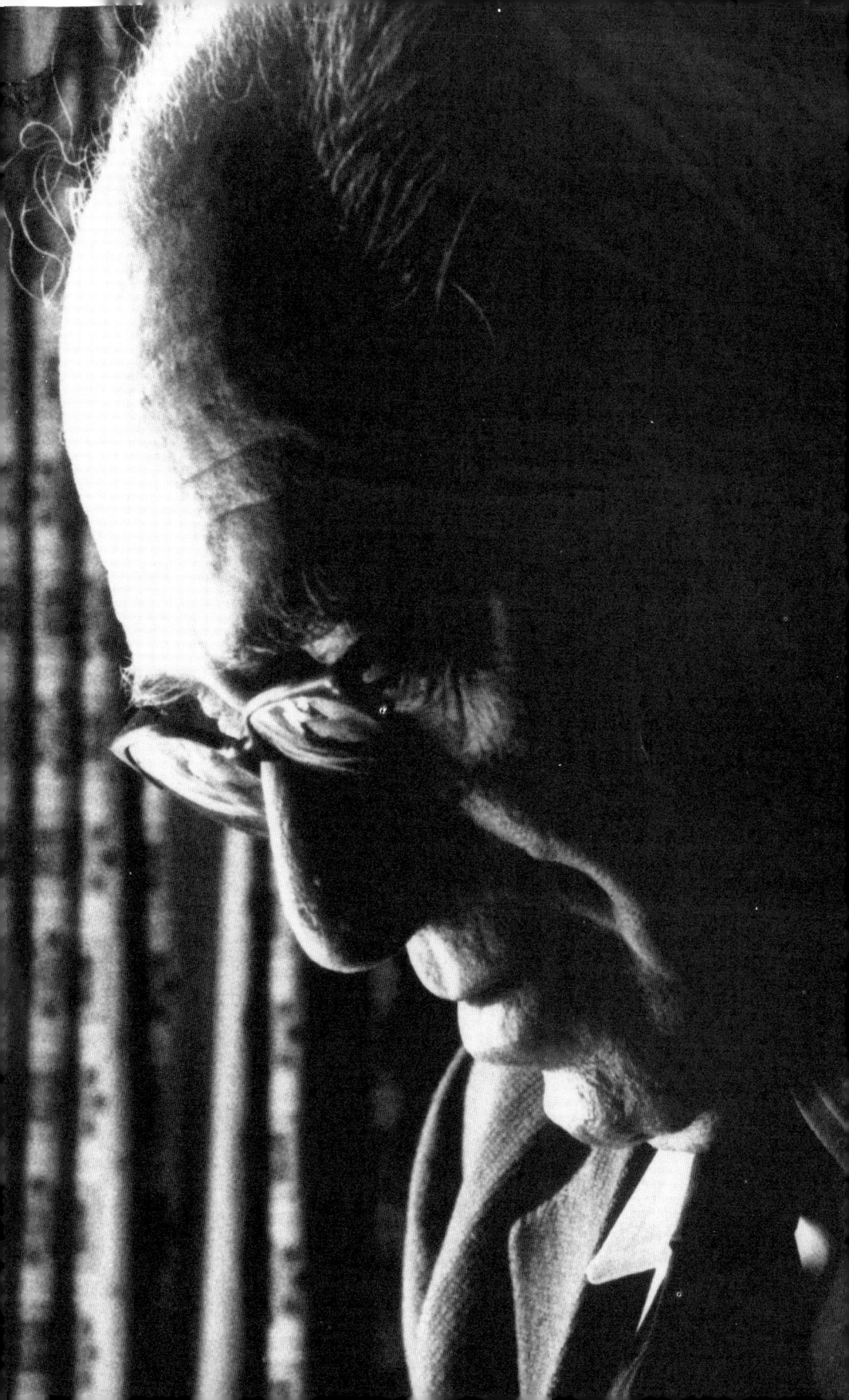

UNE FEMME AU VOLANT (A Woman at the Wheel)

(1933) Films RP, France.

Directors: Kurt Gerron and Pierre Billon; *Screenplay*: Emeric Pressburger

MON COEUR T'APPELLE (My Heart is Calling You)

(1934) Cine-Allianz Tonfilm, France.

Directors: Carmine Gallone and Serge Veber; *Screenplay*: Emeric Pressburger (German version *Mein Herz ruft nach Dir*)

MONSIEUR SANS-GENE

(1935) Amora Film, France.

Director: Karl Anton; *Screenplay*: Emeric Pressburger and René Pujol (Remade in US as *One Rainy Afternoon* directed by Rowland V. Lee)

LA VIE PARISIENNE

(1935) Néro-Film, France.

Director: Robert Siodmak; *Screenplay*: Emeric Pressburger, Benno Vigny and Marcel Carré, based on the operetta by Meilhac and Halévy (English version *Parisienne Life* *Director*: Robert Siodmak; *Screenplay*: Emeric Pressburger, Anthony Kimmins and Katherin Cawdron)

THE CHALLENGE

(1938) London Films, England.

Director: Milton Rosmer; *Screenplay*: Emeric Pressburger, Patrick Kirwan and Milton Rosmer, from an original idea by Rosmer and Kirwan
Cast: Luis Trenker, Robert Douglas, Joan Gardner, Mary Clare, Fred Groves, Bernard Miles, Lawrence Baskcomb, Violet Hayward

Mountaineering saga. When a British party beat the Italians to the Matterhorn summit, the Italian guide (Luis Trenker) is called on to save a stranded Englishman (Robert Douglas).

ATLANTIC FERRY (US: Sons of the Sea)

(1941) Warner Bros. England.

Director: Walter Forde; *Screenplay*: Emeric Pressburger with Gordon Wellesley and Edward Dryhurst; *Photography*: Basil Emmott
Cast: Michael Redgrave, Griffith Jones, Valerie Hobson, Margaretta Scott, Bessie Love, Hartley Power, Milton Rosmer, Charles Victor, Felix Aylmer, Joss Ambler

An 1840 steamship race between rival companies plying for trade between England and America. Two brothers join opposing ships.

WANTED FOR MURDER

(1946) Excelsior Films, England.

Director: Lawrence Huntington; *Screenplay*: Emeric Pressburger, Rodney Ackland and Maurice Cowan, from the play by Percy Robinson and Terence de Marney; *Photography*: Max Greene

● Emeric Pressburger in 1985.

Cast: Eric Portman, Dulcie Gray, Derek Farr, Roland Culver, Stanley Holloway, Barbara Everest, Jenny Laird, Bonar Colleano, Kathleen Harrison, Moira Lister, George Carney, Wally Patch

Victor (Eric Portman), son of a public executioner, strangles a number of young women but his attempts to murder Anne (Dulcie Gray) are foiled by the local police and a lovestruck bus conductor (Derek Farr) and he drowns himself rather than be placed under arrest.

TWICE UPON A TIME

(1953) London Films, England.
Producer and Director: Emeric Pressburger; *Screenplay*: Emeric Pressburger, based on the novel *Das Doppelte Lottchen* by Erich Kästner; *Photography*: Christopher Challis (Previously filmed as *Da Doppelte Löttchen* in Germany (1951), and later remade as *The Parent Trap* by Disney in 1961. Pressburger was not involved in either version).
Cast: Jack Hawkins, Elizabeth Allen, Hugh Williams, Isabel Dean, Michael Gough, Yolande and Charmian Larthe, Walter Fitzgerald, Isabel George

The twins of a divorced couple plan to bring their parents back together again at a holiday camp in the Tyrol.

MIRACLE IN SOHO

(1957) Rank Films, England.
Director: Julian Amyes; *Producer*: Emeric Pressburger; *Screenplay*: Emeric Pressburger; *Photography*: Christopher Challis
Cast: John Gregson, Belinda Lee, Cyril Cusack, Peter Illing, Rosalie Crutchley, Ian Bannen, Billie Whitelaw, Cyril Shaps, John Cairney, Maria Burke, Barbara Archer

Her heart broken by a roadmender (John Gregson), a Soho barmaid (Belinda Lee) prays for a 'miracle' which – in the shape of a burst water main – brings him back to her.

Emeric Pressburger also worked on screenplays under the pseudonym Richard Imrie, including *Operation Crossbow* (MGM, 1965), a wartime drama directed by Michael Anderson and starring George Peppard, Tom Courtenay, John Mills, Sophia Loren, Lilli Palmer and Anthony Quayle. Also credited as screenwriters were Derry Quinn and Ray Rigby. Pressburger used the Imrie alias again on Michael Powell's *They're a Weird Mob* (Australia, 1966).

Index

References in *italic* are to illustrations

Index

Index

● The enforced idleness of Michael Powell's later years. Leaning on gates, sitting on boxes –
it all amounts to the same thing.